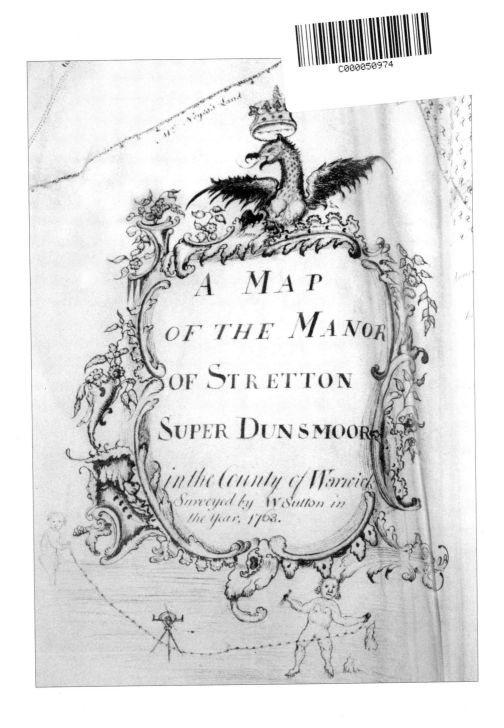

A MAP

OF THE MANOR

OF STRETTON

SUPER DUNSMOOR

in the County of Warwick
Surveyed by W. Sutton in
the Year, 1763.

STRETTON ON DUNSMORE
THE MAKING OF A WARWICKSHIRE VILLAGE

A Millennium History

STRETTON
MILLENNIUM
HISTORY GROUP

A catalogue record of this book is available from
the British Library

ISBN 0 9537462 0 8

Scanning, page make-up and typesetting by Warwick Dipple Design, Rugby.
Printed and bound in England by Eureka Press Ltd, Leicester.

This project has been made possible by grants received from
the Millennium Commission, Rugby Borough Council and Stretton Parish Council.

STRETTON ON DUNSMORE
PARISH COUNCIL

Millennium Commission

CONTENTS

Page

INTRODUCTION

The Millennium History of Stretton on Dunsmore has been produced for the whole community. This unique book is a blend of history and nostalgia; facts and reminiscences.

Throughout the book, the text is illustrated with a selection from the hundreds of photographs given to the project. In each chapter, you will find anecdotes and memories from the 20th century which relate to that subject, usually set in separate boxes for easy reference.

Whether you are a serious historian or just interested in learning more about our village, we hope you enjoy reading the book. We know you will learn a great deal about the story of Stretton on Dunsmore.

PREFACE

M any have thought of writing a history of Stretton on Dunsmore, many have gathered notes but the task had never been completed. On September 1st 1998 a group of villagers - Jesse Quinney, Denise Hume, Bryan Sapwell, Brian Clay, Sue Higgins, Freda Leaver, Rob Hume and Roger Clemons - met to discuss such a project. They brought with them a wide range of individual skills and knowledge and were later joined by Warwick Dipple, who designed the layout and prepared the book for printing.

THE AIMS OF THE PROJECT

The aims of the project were relatively simple: to produce a record, in book form, of the origins and development of the community through the ages. The plan also included an exhibition of documents and photographs and a permanent archive which would ultimately be accessible to all members of the public. A longer term aim was to increase and update archive material for future generations.

Financial support was given by the Parish Council and Rugby Borough Council and the project was included in the town's successful application for a Millennium Commission grant. Extra assistance in research and reading was provided by Anne Langley, Chris Holland, Roger Hillman and Kath Edwards. Ian Tresadern and Sophie Bramall provided additional photographic and technical support.

Such a project would not have been possible without the support of the community.

The co-ordinating panel, from left to right, front row; Sue Higgins, Jesse Quinney, Denise Hume, Freda Leaver - back row; Warwick Dipple, Bryan Sapwell, Brian Clay, Rob Hume and Roger Clemons.

Photograph by Alan Pinder

ACKNOWLEDGEMENTS

THE CO-ORDINATING PANEL WOULD LIKE TO THANK ALL THOSE WHO CONTRIBUTED IN ANY WAY TO THE PRODUCTION OF THIS BOOK. PARTICULAR THANKS GO TO:

John Anderton

Rodney Boneham

Mr E Borsley

Rev Gerald Brough (Rev. Squires' notes)

John Burden

Paul Burton

Harold Campion

Annabelle Cleaver (née Gilbert)

Ted Cramp

David Eadon

June Edmans

Ted Edwards

Mary Ferrier

Eileen Flett

Trevor Forsythe

Colin Franklin

Mrs Elizabeth French

Mrs B Gillan

Mary Hamilton

Derrick Hart

John Hartley

Ivy Healey

Maureen Hinton

Emma Hinton

Heinz Kittendorf

Knightlow School

Mr & Mrs O. Manley

Mr & Mrs Stuart Martin (USA)

Sarah Miles

Avril Moore

Wendy Morron

Tom Nix

David Oldham

Florrie Paget

Linda & Phil Parnell

Harold Parrott (USA)

Mary Pinchen

Alan Pinder

Sigi Power

Jennifer Poxon (née Hartley)

Peggy & Gordon Richardson

Janice Robinson

Bill Shields

Ian Smith

Joyce & Steve Smith

Mary Summerton

Colin Truslove

Kath & Steve Turvey

Nellie Welch

William & Margaret Wise

Paul Whitby

Alan Wordie

Gareth Fitzpatrick and the Living Landscape Trust, Boughton House

Stretton Parish Council

The Trustees of the Stretton Charities

The Village Hall Trustees

Warwick Public Records Office

Coventry Library

ACKNOWLEDGEMENTS

PHOTOGRAPHS
"Collecting Wroth Money at Knightlow Hill, November 11th 1899" and
"Drinking the health of the Duke of Buccleuch, November 11th 1899"
reproduced by kind permission of Birmingham Library Services.

All other photographs by kind permission of
The Coventry Telegraph, The Rugby Advertiser and
the residents of the Village of Stretton on Dunsmore

MAP
1763 map of Stretton on Dunsmore, from a survey by W. Sutton
reproduced by kind permission of
His Grace, the Duke of Buccleuch and Queensberry, K.T.
and the Living Landscape Trust.

1

IN THE BEGINNING
THE ORIGINS OF THE VILLAGE

For over one thousand years there has been a community in Stretton on Dunsmore. Even at the end of the first Millennium there was an established settlement here, but the origins of our village were probably several hundred years earlier. There is no documentary evidence to indicate when the first settlers came and therefore we must view this within the general pattern for the county.

PREHISTORIC WARWICKSHIRE

The first people to inhabit the Warwickshire area lived about half a million years ago, during the Old Stone Age when the landscape was thickly wooded. This early phase of human habitation ended with the Ice Age and human groups did not return until around 10,000 years ago at the beginning of the Middle Stone Age. As the climate became warmer and the ice sheets retreated, the habitat changed and the forest was re-established. These people were hunter-gatherers and the period is characterised by the use of skillfully worked flint tools. In recent times, a flint arrow head was found in Brookside and so we might assume that at least one of these groups hunted in our part of Dunsmore Heath.

Around 6,000 years ago the hunter-gatherer way of life was replaced by the simple farming of the New Stone Age people who used fire and stone axes to make clearings in the woodland where they built farms and laid out small fields. The Bronze Age which followed was a time of change. The scattered communities were coming together into tribal groups. Farming continued to expand and by 1500 BC much of the woodland in our area had been cleared and settled.

During the Iron Age, (about 800BC to 100AD) Warwickshire was dotted with small farmsteads of thatched round houses and outbuildings. These would have been surrounded by a deep ditch to keep out wild animals. In times of trouble the population may have taken refuge in one of a number of hill forts, such as nearby Wappenbury.

ROMANO-BRITISH PERIOD

By the late Iron Age, agriculture was well established and, following the Roman conquest during the 1st century AD, the original Britons were allowed to continue farming much of the land in the county. The Roman Army undoubtedly occupied our area, constructing the Fosse Way (see Chapter 11) and a fort in Baginton, but there is little evidence that Roman-style estate farms were imposed and the process of woodland clearance continued, particularly in a part of the county known as the Feldon.

THE COMING OF THE ANGLO-SAXONS

The Feldon lies south of a line from Rugby to Shipston-on-Stour. The word Feldon comes from the Anglo-Saxon word Feld meaning 'open area' or 'field.' This suggests that, when the migrating Angles and Saxons began arriving from the east and south from around

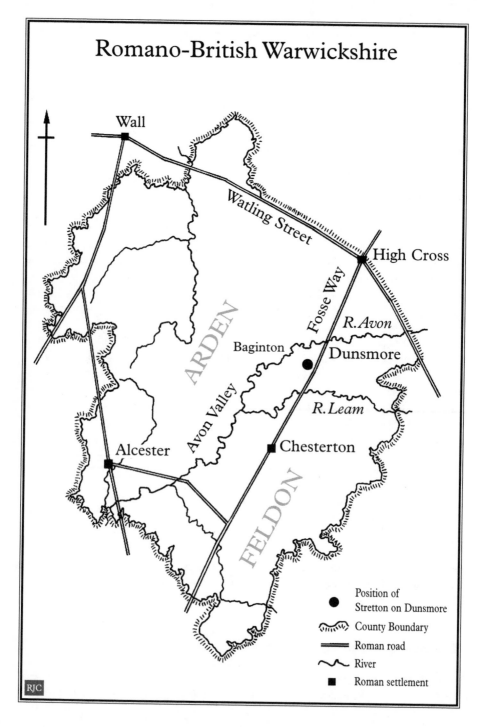

Romano-British Warwickshire

Wall

Watling Street

High Cross

Fosse Way

ARDEN

Baginton

R. Avon

Dunsmore

Avon Valley

R. Leam

Alcester

Chesterton

FELDON

● Position of
Stretton on Dunsmore

County Boundary

Roman road

River

■ Roman settlement

RJC

500 AD, they found that much of the woodland in this part of Warwickshire had already been cleared for agriculture.

They brought with them a method of farming where large fields were shared by the community living in a close-knit group. The types of village we see today with their houses concentrated around a centre, like Stretton, reflect this Anglo-Saxon domination.

THE ORIGINS OF STRETTON

Stretton is situated on the northern edge of the Feldon but, despite the existence of archaeological evidence that Stone, Bronze and Iron Age people lived close to Stretton, there appears to be no indication that the land immediately in and around the present village was farmed during those periods. The founders of the first Stretton were most probably migrating Anglo-Saxons. The name of the village is undoubtedly Anglo-Saxon, being formed from the words *straet tun on dun mor,* literally meaning "village on the road on the hill on the heath." However, recent research suggests that these groups tended to settle in areas where there were existing communities of Romano-Britons and therefore the possibility that their large fields were developed on top of earlier small enclosed fields, typical of the latter, cannot be ruled out.

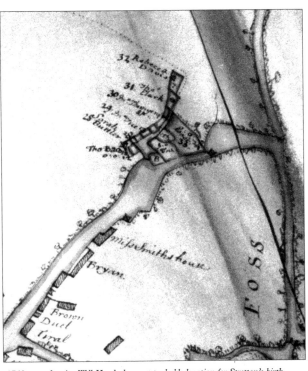

1763 map showing Well Head, the most probable location for Stretton's birth.

The first settlers would have based their decision on where to site the original community on purely practical considerations: security; the availability of fresh water; the fertility of the land. Evidence from aerial photographs suggests that the earliest mediaeval buildings were situated in the present day field which lies on the north side of Brookside where it meets the Fosse Way (grassy humps are visible from the footpath). If we take into account the nearby source of fresh water and the proximity to the Fosse Way (which would have provided access to other Anglo-Saxon groups who had settled in the Avon Valley), the most probable location for Stretton's birth is Well Head. But this can only be conjecture.

Once the initial settlement had been established, these pioneers would then have cleared enough land around their new village to provide sufficient produce to sustain the group. As the village population increased, the boundaries of the cultivated land would have been extended, with more land being claimed from the woodland or heath.

DANISH INFLUENCES

Following the invasion of England by the Danes in the 9th century, the north and east of the country were ceded to them by the Anglo-Saxons. The area under Danish control was known as the Danelaw. The frontier lay roughly along the old Watling Street (now the A5). Stretton was near the border area but there is no evidence of it being affected by the Danes. However, the name of our nearest neighbour, Princethorpe, contains the Scandinavian word *thorpe,* which usually indicates a secondary settlement and might suggest that some Danes did settle in the area. This would most likely have been with the agreement of the neighbouring Anglo-Saxon communities rather than by force of arms.

THE NORMAN CONQUEST

Following the Norman Invasion which began in 1066, the control of the country was progressively transferred from Anglo-Saxon Lords to their Norman counterparts.

Apart from the enforced change of allegiance from Saxon thane to Norman lord, it is unlikely that the lives of those early villagers would have been significantly changed by the Conquest.

> **THE DOMESDAY BOOK ENTRY FOR STRETTON**
> (translated from the original mediaeval Latin text):
>
> *"Rainald holds 5 hides in Stratone (Stretton) from Earl Roger's holding. There is land for 7 ploughs. In the demesne (lordship) there are 3 ploughs and 8 slaves; and there are 20 villeins (villagers) and 6 bordars (smallholders) with 14 ploughs. There are 5 acres of meadow. There is woodland 3 furlongs long and 1 wide. It was worth 3 pounds and afterwards 100 shillings; now 6 pounds."*

In 1086, King William ordered a survey of his new kingdom. The results were recorded in the Domesday Book.

From this we have clear written evidence that Stretton had been established before the Normans. More detail of the 'Domesday' village is given in the succeeding chapters, where we describe the social and physical changes which have occurred since that earliest record.

MEDIAEVAL EXPANSION

From the evidence available we have suggested that the village was probably first formed around Well Head. But how did the village grow from that original nucleus?

The convenient source of running water provided by the brook suggests that, as the earliest settlement expanded, additional dwellings would most probably have been located along its banks. As the population of the village rose, more and more cottages would have been added, spreading southward towards the present village centre and beyond.

Certainly the oldest cottages in the village are reputed to be those nearest the brook. Some of those we see today date back to at least the 16th century. If our proposition is correct, many are probably built on the foundations of earlier cottages built as the village expanded.

During the mediaeval period, the village's nucleus shifted from Well Head to roughly where the modern centre is today. This is indicated by three principal events.

First, a manor house of that period was built where Manor Drive now stands, directly opposite the footpath from the church. This was in ruins by the 19th century but its position is clearly shown on early maps. Even today its well beside the Shoulder of Mutton can be remembered. As late as the 1940s, animal pens, probably built from its limestone ruins, were still in use and today stone from the old manor

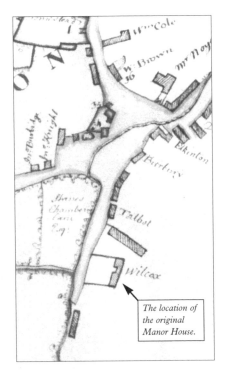

The location of the original Manor House.

Whatever its history, the moat was a favourite play area for children in the early 20th century. One of the Borsley boys wrote, "We skated on the old moat behind the church which we called the Pool Yard but for more serious skating we went to Frankton. Everyone had skates."

"The moat was eventually filled in with large quantities of debris from Coventry's blitz. When the ground was being prepared for the Curtis' house, the rubble uncovered included numerous broken toys... a poignant reminder of the wartime bombing."

can be seen at the bottom of walls at Nos. 4, 8 and 10 Brookside. The orchard behind the church may be all that remains of the old manor house gardens.

Second, a small church had been built on Church Hill. This is described in detail in Chapter 3.

Third, a large moat had been constructed to the south of the church. Its purpose is not clear but there are a number of possibilities: a moated house, a mediaeval fishpond (as at Frankton) or simply an elaborate pool in the garden of the old manor.

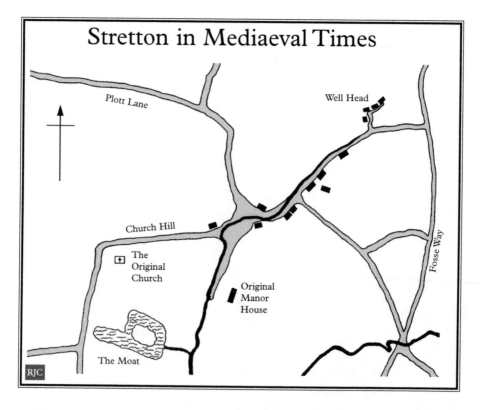

The detailed shape and size shown in 19th century maps suggest a moated dwelling rather than a fishpond or ornamental feature. The width of the water course is more than would be required to keep out animals and would clearly present a substantial defence against attack. It might therefore be suggested that this was the site of an earlier, fortified manor house, perhaps timbered and superseded by the stone manor house.

By the 15th century, Stretton had grown from the original hamlet to an established village with its own church and manor house. The changes which shaped it during the period from the 16th to the 19th century are described in Chapter 2.

2

CHANGE AND EXPANSION
THE VILLAGE FROM THE 16TH TO THE 19TH CENTURY

DEVELOPMENTS IN THE 16TH & 17TH CENTURIES

By this period, the basic layout of the village had been largely determined. The open fields had not yet been enclosed (see Chapter 8) and therefore, for simple convenience, as well as for social and security reasons, the community would most likely have lived close together in houses near to the village centre. Isolated homesteads are a feature of a later period after the land had been divided into individual farms.

In Stretton's case, the majority of houses were located along the sides of the brook from Well Head to the present centre. However, there is evidence that some cottages had also been built on Church Hill and the row of thatched cottages, which used to stand where the Shoulder of Mutton's car park is now located, may have dated from that period.

By this time, a number of villagers were becoming comparatively more prosperous than their neighbours and had begun to build themselves new houses or enlarge their existing cottages to reflect their improved economic status. Consequently, by the mid 16th century, a number of substantial properties had appeared, whereas in earlier centuries the early manor house had probably been the only notable property.

The house at Yew Tree Farm may have been the first for such improvement, followed by that at Moor Farm. Both appear to have been commenced in the 16th century.

Yew Tree Hall, as it is called, is a substantial farmhouse. The present building is comprised of four sections built at different times over a period of 300 years: reportedly 1550, 1600, 1750 and 1830.

With its double gabled front, Moor Farm is Stretton's most prominent timber-framed house. Two stone gate posts are all that remains of an imposing stone archway. It was extended over the 16th and 17th centuries. The main sitting room contains oak panelling reputed to have originated from the old church and, in its northwest wing, there is a room where the Manor Court was said to have been held, with a lock-up in a room below. The position and alignment of Moor Farm would suggest that, by the date the front was completed, the present position of the village green had already been established.

Moor Farm, Stretton on Dunsmore

In Brookside, where the entrance to Kaysbrook Drive now lies, there was another fine example of a substantial 17th century farmhouse. This was known as Parrott's House after its last owner, Walter Parrott. The original farmhouse was an L-shaped, timber-framed building with a thatched roof and walls of wattle and daub. When its use as a farmhouse ceased, it was large enough to have been divided into three or four separate households but by the 1970's the whole had fallen into disrepair. Unlike a number of village properties of the same age and condition, it was not demolished but was saved by being moved, timber by timber, to a site in Milton Keynes where it was reconstructed for use as a private house.

Another significant timber-framed house of the same period was erected in the lower part of School Lane next to Moor Farm. This building is dated 1662 and was renovated in the 1980s. Today it is known as Dunsmore House.

In Church Hill, on the right and where Stretton House now stands, there was a 17th century timber-framed house. Where the Manor House is now located, there were at that time three timber-framed cottages. Opposite them, was the old church which stood beyond the position of the present church and, on the bend at the top, you would have seen the origins of Church Farm.

16th -17th Century Stretton

The Black Dog
London Road
Frog Hall
School Lane
Fosse Way
Moor Farm
Rugby Lane
Church
Yew Tree Farm
Manor House
Moat
RJC

MORE ABOUT MOOR FARM

Moor Farm was listed as a building of special architectural or historic interest in 1951.
A timbered barn which had stood alongside it was blown down in a gale.
New mews cottages now stand on its site.

During this period, virtually all of the buildings were within the immediate village but there were two notable exceptions. On the London Road, Frog Hall and the Black Dog Inn had already been established by the 17th century.

From the original settlement through to the end of the 17th century, the changes to the physical structure of the village had evolved slowly. At the beginning of the 18th century, the village faced the dramatic change brought about by the enclosure of the common fields.

THE 18TH CENTURY VILLAGE AFTER ENCLOSURE

From about the 16th century onwards, villages began to enclose their open fields. The separated strips of land held by villagers in each of large common fields were reorganised into blocks. This formed the types of farms and small holdings with which we are familiar today.

Stretton was enclosed in 1704 (see chapter 8). Through this rearrangement of the land, the shape of the modern village was formed. Apart from new housing on the perimeter, the general area and layout of the village has not changed significantly since then. Many of the buildings which were standing at that time can still be seen today and the positions of the roads, paths and trackways closely reflect the conditions laid down in the enclosure agreement.

School Lane in the early 20th century.

The enclosure of land meant that owners now wished to live on their new holdings and a number of new farmsteads and barns arose in what were formerly open fields. Those with larger holdings appear to have been allocated land convenient to their existing houses. Without a need to move, farmhouse properties such as Yew Tree Hall were improved extensively during this post-enclosure period.

STRETTON IN THE MID-18TH CENTURY

In 1763, the Duke of Buccleuch, who owned much of Stretton, had an estate map drawn showing details of the village in that year. Some properties not owned by the Duke are omitted from the map but if we look at this map, we see that, although the general layout of the village was largely as it is today, some features are different.

The brook clearly meanders across the green, almost touching the buildings on the opposite side. There are no bridges: presumably the stream was shallow enough to be forded at will.

Moor Farm, with its impressive range of thatched barns, is already the dominant feature of the green. Where Hallmark's shop now stands, but behind the present building line, there is a shoemaker's shop. The handsome frontage was added later at the end of that century when it was bought by the Borsley family. To the rear, stands a number of small cottages and on the corner, beside the present Heydon's Cottage, we see the village blacksmith's forge.

Opposite the smithy, between Moor Farm and Dunsmore House, there is a small cottage which today no longer exists.

Look now to the other side of the green. Here, on the 1763 map, we can see the house which today is Brookside Stores. It is already in its characteristic L-shape but is detached from its neighbours. The extensions which now join it on either side have not yet been built. Facing the green, only one house in the present row is shown. This forms part of the present Brook House.

Towards Manor Drive is a further row of four cottages and beyond there is another house set back. Today this can be seen as the rear portion of No.6 Brookside. This house was originally called Stretton Farm until changed to 'Churchview' by the Reverend Townsend Powell in the 1880s.

If we look beyond this, we see the old manor house which in 1763 is occupied by the Wilcox family. Little trace of it now remains. The Shoulder of Mutton has not yet been built. A row of cottages appears just beyond its future site.

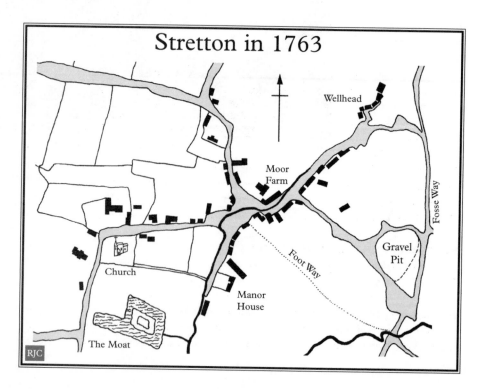

Stretton in 1763

In Church Hill there had been significant changes during the preceding century. At the top, Church Farm has grown to become one of the village's largest buildings and, opposite the old church, we see an even larger residence. This was in fact developed from the three timber-framed cottages which had stood there before. They had been cleverly joined behind a Georgian front to form a house of quality which, before mains water, even had a supply pumped up from Well Head to its own underground tanks. This is the manor house we know today.

Halfway down Church Hill, the large timber-framed house, which was there in the 17th century, is being used as the vicarage. Just below this, on the same side, we see another L-shaped house and opposite are two small cottages, located in what today forms the lower part of the churchyard. By the 19th century both the house and the cottages will have disappeared.

At the bottom of the hill, only two of the present row of cottages are shown. However, the larger house behind is already there, as too are a row of thatched cottages where Church Hill House now stands.

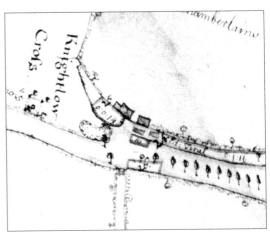

Knightlow Hill as shown in 1763.

If we follow the map to the lower part of School Lane, a row of cottages is standing on the south side and, at the corner of Plott Lane, the house of Manor Farm has already been built using bricks stamped 1760 from the kiln in Bull & Butcher Wood. These were reputedly from the same Dunchurch builder who added Borsley's new frontage.

The original map shows at least four buildings at the very end of Plott Lane. These are a group of cottages begun in the early 18th century and built on land allocated in the enclosure agreement to support the poor. The number grew steadily through the next century and the development became known as the Plott. (see Chapter 6).

At Well Head, we see an enclave of five cottages and a small shop and, along Brookside, houses and cottages line the other side as far as the centre. These areas had already been developed in earlier years and few new buildings would have been added during the 18th century. However, there is one definite addition: the original school with its attached school master's house. Today this forms No. 64 and No. 66 Brookside and was built in 1796 on land donated by a Miss Smith who lived next door, probably in Parrott's house.

On the London Road, Frog Hall is now shown as an inn. In fact a number of new cottages and inns are shown on the map, probably supported by trade from the new turnpike road. The main group of cottages are located at Knightlow Hill and appear to have been the nucleus for the later spread of housing along the highway. The inns are described in Chapter 12.

THE 19TH CENTURY VILLAGE

An early map shows how the village develops in the 19th century. Three notable architectural changes have taken place on Church Hill. The vicarage was enlarged by the Reverend William Daniel, who was vicar from 1767-1816, with the addition of its present Georgian frontage. This building ceased to be a vicarage in 1973 and is now named Stretton House.

The front of the Manor House has also been altered to its present appearance with the addition of a gabled porch and octagon bay.

Third, but by far the most significant, by 1837 the old church has been demolished and replaced with the present building.

At the top of the hill, Church Farm has grown to its present size and at the bottom the row of cottages formed by infilling the original two.

FROM THE REVEREND SQUIRES NOTES ON HIS MOVE TO THE VICARAGE IN 1956:

"A gracious house but much neglected. Evidence of dry rot in the valley between old and new. Door off landing led to 2 wings - later demolished - under floors downstairs rat infested. Sealed up back staircase near kitchen door. Dark narrow passage led from kitchen door to back door opening into the fore-court. Line of smelly buildings, wash-house, brewhouse, store, etc. Parlour maids' pantry next to kitchen. Also line of buildings in fore-court for storage of coal and coke. There was an earth closet here too. Near the back door was a deep well and pump in working order. Two other shallow wells existed, one near the open shed and the other from the garden to the kitchen garden. The newer part of the house was easily distinguishable by the architraves, skirtings and doors, also the outer brickwork. .... The main work include demolition of the two wings and 'the domestic offices', removal of the pump and filling in of the deep well. The brickwork and plastering was repaired and renewed and modern domestic facilities improved."

On the 19th century map the village green is now framed by the present buildings. A small cottage and a pound (animal enclosure) stand between Borsley's new front and the smithy on the corner. In the period since the late 1700s, the houses opposite have been extended into a row and three cottages set back to their right have replaced the earlier ones nearer the brook, with others being built behind. In the same period, a house named "The Haven" was built and 6 Brookside extended with its elegant brick frontage. The old manor is now in ruins and uninhabited but the newly-built Shoulder of Mutton appears to its right. Opposite, the Moat is still clearly visible with nearly half an acre of water around the island and no house on either side.

If we look in the other direction from the green, Moor Farm is now fully developed and the line of cottages including the Oak and Black Dog are joined into a row. Behind, Yew Tree Hall has grown to its full size and many houses are now shops. (see Chapter 9).

Brookside and Well Head appear more or less unchanged since the previous century but the first houses appear on Knob Hill.

The number of houses in the lower part of School Lane has subsequently increased. A large red-brick house named Oak Cottage has been built opposite Dunsmore House. This was used for many purposes, including a fish and chip shop, until it was demolished in the mid 20th century. A large barn, now converted to Moorbarn House, also appears on this map.

The most significant change in the lane is the appearance of the school built in 1861 in what was then Dog Lane. Beyond this is a house at the corner of the footpath to the present school. Neither of these is standing today.

At the top of Plott Lane, the houses built for the poor have increased and are now on both sides. Further down the lane the Methodist Chapel has been built.

On the London Road, the map now shows several cottages at intervals from Knightlow Hill to the Fosse Way. Virtually all on the south side were later demolished when the A45 was widened to a dual carriageway but many on the other side can still be seen today, either renovated or extended.

In this chapter, we have seen the village grow from its mediaeval roots to become, by the 19th century, a large self-supporting village. The developments of the last one hundred years are described separately in the chapters which follow.

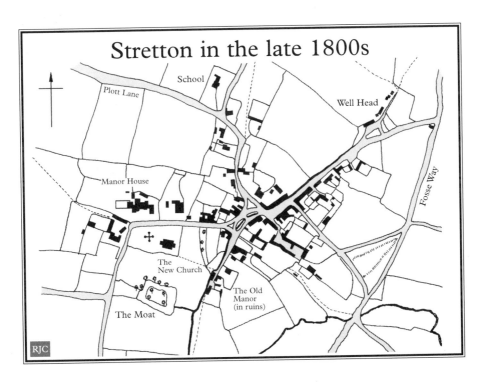

Stretton in the late 1800s

School

Plott Lane

Well Head

Manor House

Fosse Way

The New Church

The Old Manor (in ruins)

The Moat

RJC

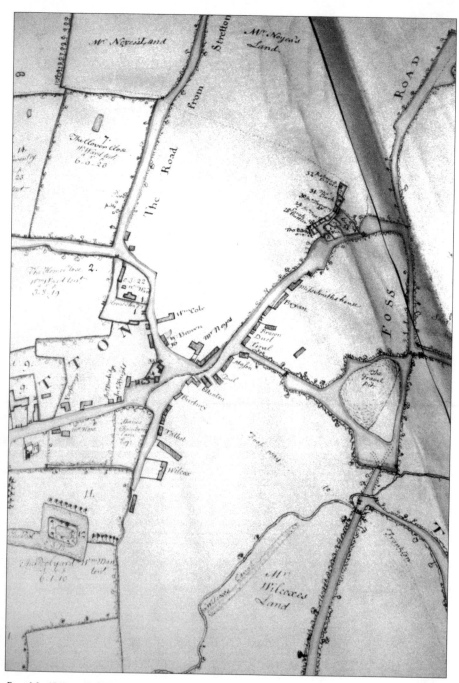

Part of the 1763 map by W Sutton.

3

GOING TO CHURCH
FAITH IN THE COMMUNITY

In this chapter we describe the church of All Saints which was consecrated in 1837 and the much older building which it replaced. We also describe the influence of the non-conformist movement in the village.

THE ORIGINAL CHURCH

Its beginnings: It is quite certain that there has been a church in the village for at least 800 years. There are no early records to provide direct evidence of this but not long before the old church was demolished in the mid 19th century, a local historian wrote of a Norman chancel, suggesting that the building was of 12th century origin. The earliest mention dates from 1321 when the records of the Lichfield and Coventry Diocese list the institution of William de Langley as priest.

The old church which was demolished in the 1830s.

THE CHANTRY CHAPEL

In 1349 there is written evidence to show that the old church had within it a special chantry or chapel. This was established by Thomas de Wolvardynton, who was priest at a church in the Leicestershire village of Lubenham and who provided two further priests to sing daily mass at the alter dedicated to St Thomas the Martyr. Such chantries were built for the offering of holy sacrifice for the benefit of souls, this one being for the souls of a number of people, including the Earl of Huntingdon. A 19th century historian described the remains of a stone altar and piscina (water basin) in the south aisle of the old church. The south aisle was also in 'decorated style,' indicating that this was built around 1350 and possibly part of the chantry which would have been added to the first Norman structure. The maintenance of the chantry appears to have lapsed, possibly as a result of the Black Death, and it was then taken over by Robert de Stretton, Bishop of Lichfield and Coventry.

THE MERGER OF STRETTON PARISH WITH WOLSTON PARISH

During the religious reformation of the 16th century, chantries were dissolved and all revenues confiscated by the Crown. During this period the parish of Stretton merged with the parish of Wolston, perhaps because the loss of church revenues made it difficult for the two to survive independently. As a result Stretton church was served by curates from Wolston for many years. The earliest registers of Stretton Church dating from 1681 record the names of Wolston clergy, Peter Haddon and Jon Stafford, officiating at the church.

A SEPARATE PARISH AGAIN

The situation changed in 1694 when William Herbert, 'gentleman of Stretton on Dunsmore', made a specific bequest of 'monies from property at Long Itchington to be used for the support of a godly and able minister to dwell in the town of Strettone and preach there every Lord's Day twice.' Two conditions were attached to the will: firstly the inhabitants of Stretton and Princethorpe were to procure an Act of Parliament to make the parish separate from Wolston; secondly, the executors of the will were 'to present a priest from time to time, when there should be a vacancy, for the approbation and liking of the major part of the inhabitants of the said town.' Such an undertaking was 'because the towns of Stretton and Princethorpe are too remote from the church [i.e. Wolston] and the inhabitants many times have not been able to repair to the same.'

An Act of Parliament was duly passed and a vicarage provided for the new incumbent. This house still exists today as the rear section and outhouses of Stretton House (see Chapter 2). The patronage of the living (the right to appoint and remunerate a vicar) was to be shared between the representatives of both William Herbert and Fisher Wentworth, the patron of Wolston church. The first vicar of this independent church was Francis Hunt, a relative of the Chamberlayne family, well-established landowners in the area. There is little recorded in the registers of those who followed him in the old church. It is possible that the next priests were not resident in the village and a curate performed the necessary services.

ALTERATIONS AND IMPROVEMENTS

In 1767 William Daniel became vicar of Stretton and did much to alter and improve both the church building and the vicarage. Firstly in 1770, 'the seats and sitting places in the parish church being insufficient to accommodate the parishioners, several of them erected, by subscription or at their own charge, a handsome gallery at the western end of the church.' Secondly, a new frontage to the vicarage was erected which enlarged the building considerably. Thirdly, he must have thought that, in spite of the new gallery, the church was too small or in bad repair because, when he died in 1816, he bequeathed the sum of £4,000, subject to the life of his widow, for the purpose of building a new church.

PROVISION OF THE LIVING

During this period of time, the Herbert share of the living had passed through the hands of the Chamberlayne family to Francis Fauquier by his marriage to Elizabeth Chamberlayne. This gentleman was to become Governor of the new world state of Virginia. The tombs of several members of the Chamberlayne family are in the churchyard, very close to the site of the old building. The communion set was presented by his son and a cousin who married in 1787. It consists of a handsome flagon, chalice and paten and bears an inscription which reads "Francis and Thermuthes Fauquier of Stoneythorpe in the County of Warwick to the parish of Stretton on Dunsmore, 1795." The set was made by J Wakelin and R Garrard. From Francis Fauquier a share of the patronage was sold to Henry Sawbridge and, on the death of William Daniel, the new incumbent was the Reverend John Silkes Sawbridge, a relative of the patron.

FURTHER IMPROVEMENTS

The new vicar seems to have worked hard to improve the old church, despite the will of his predecessor. He wrote that 'the old ceiling is pulled down and the new beam for a covered ceiling put up. This allows us to add a foot and a half to the window.' The reference relates to the installation of some mediaeval painted glass given to All Saints by a London clergyman, the Reverend Harry Norris, Rector of Hackney. Two plaques are in the present church, to Jane Sawbridge of the Manor House and to one of his twin daughters, who died in 1808. As this was before his appointment in 1817, he may have wished to save the old building because of a longer standing association with the village.

THE NEW CHURCH

A new building: In spite of his efforts, the old church must have been in bad repair: an Act of Parliament in 1832 reads *'the church or chapel of Stretton on Dunsmore being in a ruinous and dilapidated condition so as to render it expedient for the same to be wholly taken down and rebuilt.'* A new church was duly built nearby and the old one demolished. The outline of the old church can still traced on the bank to the west of the church, near the Chamberlayne tombs.

The first stone of the new church was laid in 1835.

17

"The bells in the old wooden steeple called up the villagers on Whit Tuesday morning to prepare for a scene that had never before that day been known in Stretton... I can fancy myself in the very act of admiring the care with which Mr Marriott smoothed the mortar with his silver trowel...seeming to join with all his heart in the prayer which followed.

May God give His blessing on this good work which is now begun to the glory of his name."

The stone from the old church was re-used to form part of the wall between the Manor House and the old vicarage. The bells, bell frame and the mediaeval glass were all used in the new building and several monumental plaques also resited.

The land for the new building was obtained from John Clark Powell of Bishopsgate, London, who had obtained the Fisher Wentworth share of the patronage (as explained earlier in this Chapter) at a cost of *'ten shillings of lawful money.'* The funds for the new building were to come from the bequest of the Reverend William Daniel.

The event took place in the reign of William IV and Queen Adelaide whose effigies were carved in stone in the corbels under the drip mould of the East window. Two years later, again on Whit Tuesday, an estimated 5000 people came for the consecration of the new church. The bands played, streamers were waved and, as the Reverend Powell said, *"the glorious work is accomplished. May the Lord give it his blessing."* It had been built at a cost of £5,232.

THE DESIGN

The new church was designed by Thomas Rickman in a Gothic Revival style: an imposing building built with stone from Attleborough near Nuneaton and lined with brick and plaster. The tower was originally surmounted by four decorated pinnacles and a tracery pinnacle. This was over 70 feet (22 metres) high. In 1903, however, one of the pinnacles was blown down. Sadly the remaining three were levelled to match.

Inside the building the architect used pre-cast concrete for the prayer desk, pulpit, font, gallery front and other features, introducing new materials as an alternative to those traditionally used. The pillars and vaulting rise 35 feet (11 metres) to the nave roof and there is no chancel but an apse or sanctuary in its place.

No two window headings are alike. The window on the south sanctuary wall contains the mediaeval glass from the old building. The stained glass in the large east window was installed in 1936 as a gift from Captain and Mrs Charles Stiff of Wolston Grange. The artist was Donald Taunton of Edgbaston and the work carried out in Hardman's Studios in Birmingham. The All Saints design shows a centre panel of Christ ascending, surrounded by other panels depicting a number of saints, principally St Augustine of Canterbury and St Osbourg of Coventry. Running across the window is the scroll *'We praise thee O Lord, we acknowledge thee to be the Lord.'*

The clerestory windows feature circles filled with foils and mouchettes (decorative shapes). In the corners of the sanctuary are panels showing angels which were painted by Mr Norman, an ecclesiastical artist from Warwick. The memorial plaques include several from the old church and notably that to the Reverend William Daniel, the main instigator of the new church.

> *"During the Rev. Ward's time, the church clock had been stopped for some time. He asked the Parish Council for help who found that it was cheaper to have the clock converted to electric than to have it mended. The clock was previously wound by hand."*
>
> *"In earlier times there were lanterns at the gate and lamps in church. These were prepared and lit for each service."*

THE BELLS

The earliest written record of bells in Stretton on Dunsmore is in an inventory compiled by the Commissioners of Edward VI in 1552 in which Stretton is listed as having *"iij great belles, a saunce bell, iij small belles and two handbells."* The origins of these are not clear, although it is thought that they could have come from the old priory in Wolston. As Stretton was part of the parish of Wolston until 1696, this may well be true. The old church was demolished in 1835 and records show that three bells were transferred in their old frame to the tower of the new church in 1837.

THE BELL RESTORATION PROJECT

It is not known when these three bells had been last rung in traditional manner but after 1939 the wooden frame had become so decayed that the bells were only chimed.

In 1989 a plea from the then vicar, Gerald Brough, for the bells to be rung again resulted in a group of six people volunteering to learn the art of chiming. The six volunteers soon decided to form their own committee, led by Paul Burton, to explore the idea of a full renovation and in 1989 the Bell Restoration Project was born. The estimated cost of the scheme for a new eight bell steel frame and six bells, to include two of the originals, was £35,000; this did not include the considerable amount of restoration work required to the inside of the tower itself.

> **STRETTONS SOLE BELL RINGER –**
>
> *"In 1954 George Paget was recorded as sole bell ringer, ringing three bells at once – a rope in each hand and one loop over his foot! In the same year he also celebrated 69 years as a church chorister."*

THE RE-CASTING

In 1991 the old bells were finally moved to the Whitechapel Foundry. The treble and the second bells had been cast in 1705 by Joseph Smith, Warwickshire's first bell-founder. On examination, the old second bell was found to be unsuitable for the restoration scheme. Its inscription was recorded as follows:

> JAMES ELKINGTON AND THOMAS BROMAGE
> CHURCH WARDINGS 1705

The tenor bell, however, cast by Hugh Watts II of Leicester in 1620, was found to be suitable for use as the tenor in the new frame. March 1992 saw the casting of the first new bell - "The Ray Bell" - to be donated in memory of a well-known villager, Ray Nichols, who died suddenly and tragically in October 1990.

By October 1992 the new frame was fitted and the three bells raised. Lacking wheels and fittings,

Ann Henshaw and Veronica Nichols fundraising for the new bells.

these were still not ready to use but were sufficient to increase the momentum of the project and generate further funds. On Christmas morning 1992 the three bells were rung full circle for the first time.

Early in 1993 a further bequest allowed the purchase of another bell and the start of regular ringing practices for the team of ringers. Finally, extra fund-raising efforts meant that the last two bells could be cast and hung in February 1994.

Old Tenor Bell on its headstock.

The Rev. Stanley Collier enjoyed boxing and always had a pair of boxing gloves in the vicarage. On one occasion he was threatened by an angry parishioner who experienced a priestly punch which floored him!

The Rev Collier would stand no nonsense and, according to legend, was able to "box a child's ears and kick his backside at the same time."

The Reverend S.G. and Mrs Collier outside the vicarage in the 1920s.

The full ring of six bells was dedicated in a service on April 16th 1994. The completion of the project is a tribute to the many people who have worked together with a common aim. The sound of the bells floating over the village before Sunday service is a mark of the commitment of Stretton bellringers past and present.

The Rev. Squires was a keen historian and researched much of the history of the parish which is included in this chapter.
In his notes he records that he suffered a disappointing arrival to the parish with no-one to welcome him and his wife, apart from two non-conformists.

THE COMMUNITY AT WORK

The scheme soon became a community project and in 1991 sufficient funds were in place, from active fund-raising by villagers, donations, legacies and grants, to start work.

Almost every weekend over a period of three years, a team of volunteer workers dismantled the old frame, fitted the new structure and strengthened the tower to receive the old and the new bells. A lifting arrangement, specially designed by Stretton engineer James Wallace, who also supervised the construction work, allowed easy access to the tower and proved invaluable for raising the bells to their final position.

THE INCUMBENTS OF ALL SAINTS, STRETTON ON DUNSMORE

1321	William de Langley
1346	William de Lubenham
1349	Augustillian de Stretton
1359	Robert de Hurleye
1371	John Gibbe

Stretton then became part of Wolston parish until 1696

1696	Rev. Francis Hunt
1722	Rev. Richard Ames
1736	Rev. Rodolf Sheward
1766	Rev. William Daniel
1817	Rev. John Sikes Sawbridge
1830	Rev. Harry Townsend Powell
1855	Rev. Henry Wybrow
1880	Rev. John Richardson
1906	Rev. Stanley Collier
1941	Rev. Owen Ward
1952	Rev. James Paterson Ferguson
1956	Rev. William Squires
1970	Rev. John William Roberts
1973	Rev. Gerald Brough
1993	Rev. Robert Rogers
1998	Rev. Christine Pollard

RECENT CHANGES

Normal maintenance and some renewal has kept the new church building in good condition ever since. Some of these works are worthy of mention:

In the late 1970s, the relatively unusual facility of a toilet was installed, partly as a result of family services attended by many young children.

The Church Bell Restoration Team.

In 1987, the interior of the church was beautifully redecorated by a group of unemployed young men. The cost of their supervision and training was covered by a government employment assistance scheme.

The building was subsequently rededicated in a moving service. A flower festival followed to celebrate the 150th anniversary of the new church and, as at the original opening, this was marked by a rendering of the Hallelujah chorus by a specially formed choir.

In 1973 the church was once again to share a priest with two other villages - Frankton and Bourton.

The first priest to serve the joint benefice was Gerald Brough. The present incumbent, Christine Pollard, is also breaking new ground as the first female vicar in the history of Stretton church.

THE BELLS ARE INSCRIBED AS FOLLOWS:	
Treble	The Bell Restoration Team, May 1991-Dec 1993
2nd	In memory of Lily Poole 1900-1993
3rd	In loving memory of Ray Nichols 1942-1992
4th	JOSEPH SMITH IN EDGBASTON MADE MEE 1705
5th	Gerald Brough Vicar 1977-1993 *In acknowledgement of his commitment to the parish.*
Tenor	IHS; NAZARENVS REX.IV DEORVM FILI DEI MISERERE MEI 1620 *Cast by Hugh Watts of Leicester 1620*

NON-CONFORMIST MOVEMENTS

The beginnings of dissent.

From the 17th century onwards, non-conformist Christian groups developed, expressing dissent from the theology and practice of the established Anglican church. The nearest and earliest known group in the Stretton area was a baptist movement at Wolston. In 1818 their minister, Mr George Jones, came to Stretton to preach at open air gatherings. This caused anger amongst the Anglicans, leading to the appearance of the vicar of All Saints at one such meeting, telling the congregation to follow him, "the only authorised shepherd." He was unsuccessful and further gatherings continued in the village both in and out of doors. In 1820 at a gathering in a cottage in Plott Lane, churchwardens, constables and parochial officers appeared to interrupt the meeting and fighting broke out. Injury to the householder resulted in the parish officers being tried and found guilty of assault at Warwick Assizes.

"When I passed the chapel in Plott Lane I always removed my hat, as a sign of respect, or risk receiving a 'four-penny one' from my elder brother."

22

In the early 19th century, the Primitive Methodists in Rugby initiated a movement to return to their Wesleyan roots and began preaching out of their churches to 'spread the gospel.' One Rugby inhabitant affected by this was a chimney sweep named Elijah Cadman who became a convert after renouncing his vices in a misspent youth. He formed the 'Hallelujah Band' from a group of ten young men who dressed in red shirts and travelled around the villages to preach in the open air. His impact on Stretton was such that his name appears as a trustee of the Methodist Chapel which was later formed in the village.

> *Miss Jones, an organist for many years, lived in Rugby and cycled to chapel in Stretton until she was 70, changing her clothes on arrival.*

THE FIRST METHODIST CHAPEL

The local Methodist leader was Mr Howard who lived in a house behind what is now Toadstool Cottage in Brookside (facing Church Hill). Opposite his cottage was a long low building, which was used for worship by Methodists at the end of the 19th century. However, it was not sufficiently suitable and a replacement was soon required. The building was known for many years as "the old Chapel" and still exists today in private use.

> *If the visiting Minister was taking afternoon and evening service, he would stay at Mrs Healey's for tea and then take evening service. The same Mrs Healey worked hard to keep the chapel going. When she died the congregation declined and the chapel closed.*

THE CHAPEL IN PLOTT LANE

In 1871 a small new chapel was built on a strip of the waste land known as 'the Slang' in Plott Lane. In keeping with the Primitive Methodist tradition, it was a simple, unadorned building. Two years after its opening, it was enlarged to hold the increasing number of families attending the services. Mr Howard continued to lead the congregation and was a founding trustee.

The services were mostly led by preachers from outside the village. To allow for this, the services were held at 3pm and 6.30pm, with hospitality provided in between. Mr Smith, a shepherd from Easenhall, became an accredited preacher in

Methodist Chapel in Plott Lane, Stretton.

View of the Church from the Fosse Way. The cottages, now demolished stood on what is now the Shoulder of Mutton car park.

1874 and walked from his home and back again to preach at Stretton. The village continued to 'entertain' visiting ministers although in the 1930s Charlie Capp and Percy Smith, who lived in the village, also took many services.

Many local children were christened at the chapel and funerals were also conducted, although burial was in the village churchyard. The only restriction to its function was marriage: with no appropriate licence, weddings were not possible at the chapel.

Children who went to chapel also attended the local church aided school, some singing in All Saints church choir and also attending the afternoon Methodist service. Adults were either 'church' or 'chapel' but never both.

THE DEMISE OF THE CHAPEL

After the death of Mr Howard, the work of the trusteeship rested firstly with his two unmarried daughters, Lily and Mary and later with Mrs Healey. Attendance declined for many reasons and as transport improved many villagers eventually preferred to worship in larger chapels in Coventry. In the early 1970s, the lack of leadership and trustees led to its closure. The building still remains and is used for storage.

4

MANOR AND PARISH
CIVIL ADMINISTRATION, LAW AND ORDER

A village is not just a collection of houses, it is a community and, as an assortment of people, buildings and activities, requires administration and organisation. In this chapter, we focus on these aspects of Stretton since mediaeval times and describe the social changes which have occurred since the earliest records.

THE FIRST RECORDS

Before the Norman Conquest, the villages of Wolston and Stretton were ruled by the same Anglo-Saxon chief. He was Almund and was the earliest named individual to have held land at Stretton.

The first picture of the social structure in the village comes directly from the Domesday Book in 1086. This great survey conducted at the instruction of William the Conqueror recorded the details of the people and the entry for Stretton is shown in full in Chapter 1.

At the time of the Domesday Book, the two villages continued to be linked: they were both held by Roger de Montgomery, Earl of Shrewsbury. As one of William the Conqueror's loyal followers, he had been granted several large estates throughout the country. He appointed his own followers as lords of the many manors he owned, granting Stretton and Wolston to Rainald de Bailleul.

At that time there are estimated to have been 130 men, women and children living in Stretton. The manor was a feudal agricultural community over which the lord had absolute authority. Below him, there were broadly three social levels. Each of these groups were obliged to work on the lord's land but to differing degrees. The first and highest group were the villeins: in Stretton there were 20 such men and their families who would have been allocated a share of land in the open fields (typically 15-30 acres) in return for one or two days labour per week. The second group were six families of 'bordars' or smallholders who were allowed less land, possibly half as much, but were required to do more work for their lord than the villeins. Finally, there were the lowest class of all: eight 'serfs' or slaves who had no land and worked exclusively on the estate. These may have been condemned criminals or even prisoners taken in battle but they are more likely to have been unpaid servants who had 'sold themselves' to the lord in return for security and to avoid starvation.

SOCIAL CHANGE THROUGH THE MEDIAEVAL PERIOD

The manor continued to be ruled by lords through the mediaeval period and the duty of the villagers to provide labour continued. The life of a typical villager in the 13th century was probably not a lot different to that in 1086. The main exception would have been the gradual replacement of serfdom with an emerging class of agricultural labourers and an increase in the villein class. But despite these changes, by modern standards, the villagers were still only half-free because of the feudal rights which the lord of the manor held over them.

THE DESCENT OF THE MANOR

pre 1066	**Almund** - the last Anglo-Saxon chief over Stretton and Wolston
1086	**Rainald de Bailleul** - as tenant of Roger de Montgomery, Earl of Shrewsbury - also held Wolston
1235	**John Fitzalan** - also held Wolston and Church Lawford
1242	**Ralph Strange** - followed by his heir
c1250	**Thomas de Garshale & his wife Maud**
1262	**Robert Heriz** of Stretton - transferred by Thomas & Maud for 20 marks in silver and a rent of 1d or a pair of white gloves
c1265	**Henry de Hastings** - transferred by Robert Heriz for 30 marks and the same rent
1313	**The Hastings family** sublet part of Stretton, creating a second manor

ORIGINAL MANOR

*Original manor remained with the **Hastings** family, but the descent is unclear until:*

1656   4th Earl of Southampton - succeeded by his daughter, **Elizabeth** who married Lord Percy, later the Duke of Northumberland. Her second husband was **Ralph, 1st Duke of Montagu.**

John, 2nd Duke of Montagu - succeeded from Ralph. He married Mary Churchill, daughter of 1st Duke of Marlborough.

Their granddaughter Elizabeth married **Henry, the 3rd Duke of Buccleuch** and **5th Duke of Queensberry**

NEW MANOR

*New manor held by **Thomas de Bray** and his wife **Alice** and held by the Brays for more than 100 years, passing to the Starkey family and their descendants through the marriage of Helen to **Edmund Starkey** in the 15th C.*

1562   William Starkey sold to **Anne Longueville**, widow of Sir Thomas. Estate inherited by her sons, **Bartholomew** and **Anthony Tate** and grandson, **George Tate**.

1620   Richard Taylor of Binley - purchased from George Tate. Remained in the Taylor family for over a century.

c1750   William and Mary Butler - succeeded Samuel Taylor who was Mary's brother.

1759   George, Earl of Halifax - purchased from the Butler family.

MANOR REUNITED

1771	**The manor reunited** - The 3rd Duke of Buccleuch, who had already inherited one part of the old manor, also inherited the second part from George, Earl of Halifax. Land in Stretton remained with the Dukes of Buccleuch and Queensberry until modern times.

It is unlikely that the population would have changed a great deal in the Middle Ages. It probably grew slowly but we have no record of precise figures for this period: most mediaeval statistics were approximations and based on tax payers or property owners rather than actual population. However, such a tax listing in 1332, the Lay Subsidy Roll for Warwickshire, names eighteen property owners in Stretton who owned goods sufficient to be taxed; anyone having goods worth less than ten shillings was exempt. This represented a significant sum in those days and indicates that the village had an increasing number of more prosperous inhabitants. If we estimate that these represented 20% of the village and that the average family size was five, there would have been around 350 villagers living in Stretton in the 14th century.

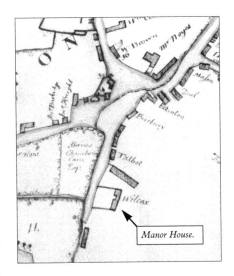

Manor House.

Copy of part of the 1763 map showing original manor house.

PARISH RECORDS - 16TH, 17TH AND 18TH CENTURIES

Records of burials have been kept in Stretton since 1681 and of marriages and births since 1695. Prior to this, records were listed under Wolston Parish with little indication of precise location.

Spelling in the records varied as most villagers would not have been able to write and relied on the recorder. As handwriting was sometimes barely legible, the spelling of family names changed as the years went on.

SOME OF THE ENTRIES IN EARLY RECORDS SHOW NAMES WHICH BECAME FAMILIAR IN STRETTON OVER THE FOLLOWING CENTURIES. THEY MAY WELL HAVE BEEN IN THE VILLAGE EVEN EARLIER:

1560	*Hart, Parott, Hinton, Herbert, Lissaman*
1620	*Elkington, Stone*
1694	*Clarke, Bacon, Wilkinson, Lucas, Tarbert, Watson*
1719	*Wilcox*
1724	*Paget, Turrell, Mann*
1755	*Kendall*
1756	*Quinney, Gilbert*
1759	*Coleman*
1764	*Boneham*

In the earlier part of the 17th century, children were recorded simply under their father's name - for example, daughter or 'fount' (son) of William Herbert. Around 1627 records started to include the mother's name.

> *"Burial records for Stretton also record the practice of 'burial in wool'. To improve the wool trade, it was decreed by Parliament in 1678 that no corpse (except those who had died of the plague) should be buried in anything other than pure sheep's wool.*
> *A certificate to that effect accompanied each interment and was recorded for many years in the village burial registers from 1681.*
> *The decree remained in force until 1825."*

In general, parish records for the village are no different to any other parish in the country. However, there appear to have been a considerable number of marriages at Stretton in the 17th and 18th century where neither party came from the parish. According to research by the Reverend Squires in the 1950s, Stretton appears to have been a favourite place for secret marriages which were not uncommon at that time for reasons of politics, property and social pressure. Around 1753 various laws were passed to prevent this practice.

POPULATION IN THE 19TH AND 20TH CENTURY

Records of population are readily available from the 19th century onwards. In 1811 the village contained 135 houses and 634 inhabitants. The 1841 census listed a population of 660 plus 25 boys and adults at the Warwick County Asylum in Frankton Lane.

By 1900 a population of 668 people is recorded and this remained roughly the same until World War II when the absence of various members of the community reduced it to 648.

The census in 1961 showed a rise to 919 and in 1991 a further increase to 1,191.

> *"The Asylum had been established in 1818 on the site of the present Hill Farm and housed boys aged between fourteen and sixteen years who had been convicted as criminals in the county. Here they were kept for two years, under the control of a warden and his wife, making shoes and clothes. It closed between 1861 and 1871."*

SOCIAL STATUS IN THE 19TH & EARLY 20TH CENTURY

The days of the lord of the manor had long gone but even at the end of the 20th century, memories are still strong of the 'gentry' and in particular the Lister-Kaye family who occupied the Manor House for many years. They employed a large number of people and at one time, several of the back row pews were occupied entirely by the staff of the Manor. In addition to having the first car in the village and holding offices on several village trusts and committees, the family had a further important claim to fame in hosting an interesting marriage.

28

A MARRIAGE OF DISTINCTION AUGUST 9 1893 – ALICE WILSHIRE - PATRICK BOWES-LYON

"Alice Wilshire was the daughter of an ex-miner and came from a small village in the Rhondda Valley. On leaving Wales to work in London at the age of 21, she met Patrick Bowes-Lyon, son of the 14th Earl of Strathmore. A romance flourished and a sympathetic friend of the young nobleman, Captain Arthur Lister-Kaye, made Alice his ward and brought her to Stretton to live with his wife and family. She was sent to finishing school in Europe and two years later the young couple were married in Stretton. The union was clearly accepted and the wedding was attended by the Bowes Lyon family with a large number of guests. A red carpet is said to have been laid the length of Church Hill. Alice became a great favourite of the family and ultimately aunt to the present Queen Mother."

LOCALS WERE NOT ALWAYS COWED BY 'GENTRY':

"Old Ned Grant was a character at the start of the century. Once driving his cart loaded with brushwood along the London Road, 'one of those new-fangled cars' came along. As it passed the cart, the wood scratched the shining new paint. The driver got out, furious, and demanded to know his name at which Ned, producing a 7lb axe from the front of the float, replied "Tell 'ee what, I'll print it on your forehead!"
The driver decided not to pursue the matter.

LAW AND ORDER

There are few references to law and order in Stretton in the middle ages, except for an important reference in 1348 to John, son of the parson of Lubenham, who was indicted for murder while living in Stretton. His link with the village can be seen in Chapter 3, where William de Lubenham is listed a vicar in 1346.

In 1696 Stretton, which had been part of Wolston, became its own parish with separate records. Among the 17th century records of the Warwickshire Quarter Sessions are many references to petty offences in Stretton. On one occasion, however, the whole parish was fined for not keeping roads and bridges in proper repair. There are also records of people trying to evade 'parish dues'.

With no police force until the 19th century, the parish and the lords of the manor would have been responsible for law and order in the village and anyone offending would ultimately be brought before the courts. Some of the more interesting entries from the Quarter Session records give an insight into village life.

LAW AND ORDER IN STRETTON: SOME ENTRIES FROM THE QUARTER SESSION RECORDS -

1650   Ralph Taylor appointed constable of Stretton super Dunsmore (a constable at that time was appointed to maintain the security of the parish and muster arms and men in the event of war).

Mr Jacob Jefcott, minister of Stretton, refused to pay the constable's levies. The court directed that, although he was minister, he should still pay his dues.

1658   Mr Jefcott, ordered by the court to pay his proportion of a levy made for the purpose of casting a bell.

1692   A warrant issued for the apprehension of Richard Russell to answer the charge of begetting a bastard child.

1693   Elizabeth Johnson presented as a common scold, a nightwalker and alleged to have "made a song or ballad in derision of her uncle and his son in the night."

1694   Katherine Watson alleged to have said she would burn her neighbour's house down and presented as a common scold.

1829   The London Road provided the setting for a dramatic event when guards on the "Eclipse" coach carrying convicts on their way for transportation to Botany Bay were overpowered by the desperate men. All were subsequently recaptured, except for two forgers who were never heard of again.

1891   George Clarke, innkeeper at the Shoulder of Mutton Inn, charged with supplying liquor during prohibited hours. On entering the house at a quarter to midnight, PC Eckford found a man who had gone there to assist in serving, and another named Nicholas. A woman also present was said to be merely a travelling hawker who "had simply gone in to buy a bottle of soda."

PC Anderton

LAW AND ORDER IN THE 20TH CENTURY

The old police house was situated opposite the Dun Cow (now Crazy Daisy's nightclub) next door to the old Black Dog Inn. The new police house was built before the Second World War at the junction of Freeboard Lane and the London Road. Both houses are now private houses.

In the early part of the century, policemen were not allowed to use bicycles and were forced to walk their 'beat'. Stretton's PC Anderton would start off from the police house, walk towards Dunchurch to make contact with their village policeman, on to Princethorpe where he would meet the Marton policeman, through Ryton and Willenhall to meet with their policemen and finish the circuit in Stretton. If

1836 THE MURDER OF THOMAS WEST

"In the spring of 1836 Stretton was the scene of a violent murder. For four years this remained unsolved until a witness, James Cooper, while serving sentence for his own crimes, made a solemn statement in 1840 on board the transportation ship 'The Leviathan' at Portsmouth.

While making his way home along Dog Lane (now School Lane) from an inn at Wolston, the witness had overheard sounds of a scuffle on the London Road, which he described as being by Dudley's beer shop, a cottage then opposite Frog Hall. Returning to the road, he saw two men fighting in the road and a third man, named Oldham, standing behind a tree. As he watched, he became aware that the two struggling men were Thomas West, a horsekeeper who looked after coach horses in the village, and George Watts, a lodger with the Allington family. The latter now seemed to be raining blows on Thomas West with an iron hammer. As Cooper drew near the onlooker, the body became still and Cooper heard Oldham tell the assailant to drag the body into the road

'so that the coach will go over him.'

During the ensuing conversation, Oldham told Cooper that the quarrel had been over Allington's wife and begged Cooper not to mention the subject or both he and Watts would both be hanged. Cooper apparently did not speak of the matter until 1840, by which time George Watts had enlisted in the 6th Regiment of Foot, embarking for Bombay on June 5th 1839."

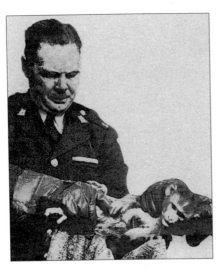

PC George Forsythe keeps his gauntlets on when handling a captured circus monkey.

transport was required to take prisoners to Rugby, a pony and trap was used. In earlier times, a small room at the side of Moor Farm was occasionally used as a makeshift prison. Eventually with the advent of modern communication, the police house was one of the first buildings in the village to have a telephone.

In the 1950s PC George Forsythe recorded a number of interesting stories in Stretton, despite its quiet location. On one occasion an overturned circus van at Ryton gave rise to a lively chase across local fields in the hunt for 50 escaped monkeys. Several days later all but three had been found and these were eventually recovered by the persistent constable.

A second story from the constable's records tells of a phantom lorry which drove headlong at other vehicles, only to vanish at the moment of impact so that astonished drivers swerved off the road. One particular evening, when icy conditions had caused a pile-up on the London Road, the officer himself saw the large vehicle pass right through the wreckage and through fires which had been lit as a warning.

Constable Forsythe was later promoted to superintendent and awarded the MBE for pacifying angry rioters in Cyprus.

THE MODERN VILLAGE

In the 1980s the Neighbourhood Watch scheme was introduced into the village. A committee drawn from various areas of the village communicates regularly with the area police station at Wolston. Despite a slight increase in crime and occasional 'incidents', the village still records a crime rate well below the local average.

The practical duties of maintaining the modern village are now undertaken by our systems of local government.

Stretton in the early 1980s

> *"Jack Kennedy was a particularly prominent chairman of the Parish Council before his death at a relatively young age. In 1971 his wife commissioned an insignia designed, as a memorial, for the Chairman of the council to wear. John Ragsdale, a local designer, created the unusual and up-to-date square stainless steel medallion, suitably inscribed, to be worn on a green ribbon."*

THE PARISH COUNCIL

Local government in some form has existed for centuries, administered through the manor and the parish, as described earlier in this chapter and Chapter 6. By the mid-19th century, the power of the manor and Church had diminished and this administrative system had been reduced to a bare minimum. The Local Government Act introduced by Gladstone in 1894 effectively excluded the Church from formal participation in local government and created the basis for the modern parish council.

Today, Stretton Parish Council works with the County and Borough Councils to supervise and control a variety of administrative areas. Over the last 20 to 30 years the Stretton council have been involved in a number of major issues, including the monitoring of sand and gravel extraction at Frog Hall quarry and of proposed and actual housing developments. They have also played a significant role in safety improvements on the A45. A campaign to look after the monument and traffic island also resulted in the County Council taking responsibility for this.

In 1977 a considerable amount of money collected from celebrations for the Queen's Silver Jubilee was used to establish a new playing field in Plott Lane. A field adjacent to this has also been purchased to make provision for the eventual need for an additional burial ground.

Some of the work has been aesthetic as well as practical: in 1973, after a government initiative, council members helped to plant 75 trees around the area, mainly wild cherry, copper beech and sycamore. The village has also received a number of awards and commendations in recent years in the Best Kept Village competition. Stretton was awarded first place in the large village section for the Rugby area in 1999.

The Stretton Parish Council at the turn of the Millennium.

The conservatory and garden at The Manor House.

5

In Sickness and in Health
Health, Hygiene and the Public Services

Like all communities throughout Britain, the modern village benefits by local supplies and services. For many centuries, however, it was obliged to provide its own services to maintain the health of its inhabitants. This chapter illustrates the changes over the years.

Health Pre 20th Century

Throughout the mediaeval and later periods, the population in many parts of the country suffered considerably from plagues, fever and other infectious diseases. The earliest recorded outbreak was the plague known as the Black Death which swept through Europe in the mid 14th century. In some places populations were reduced by more than 50% and in Warwickshire several villages disappeared. Stretton survived and seemed to thrive. The parish subsequently merged with the parish of Wolston and then separated again; this may be an indication that the two villages suffered from later outbreaks of plagues.

The Black Death or bubonic plague was also the most important outbreak of disease in the 17th century. It was spread by parasites living on rats and, although there is no record that Stretton was directly affected, rats would certainly have been numerous in the early village.

From Stretton parish registers, it would appear that weather was the biggest health hazard. In 1760, of the fourteen parishioners who died, only two died in the summer. Epidemics of infectious diseases also brought more serious consequences than we know today. In 1796 and 1797 a total of 45 deaths were recorded, compared to 8 in 1798. Infant mortality was high, not only because of poor conditions at birth but also from childhood diseases such as measles and diptheria. For example, records in Frankton show the deaths of eleven children under the age of twelve in 1858 where the annual average would have been two.

> Even in living memory, rats were a part of everyday life:
> *"The cottages at Well Head had corrugated tin put on top of the thatch and you could lie in bed listening to rats or mice scuttling about. Toilets were at the end of the garden and you always kicked the bucket first to get rid of any unwelcome visitors."*

Health problems were even greater where the population was more crowded and conditions less hygienic. One such place was Rugby and even at Rugby School "the stench of cesspools" was often offensive. The result was that in 1849 the town, which would have had a direct influence on Stretton, became the first in England to form a Board of Health. A considerable improvement in survival rates is indicated in the village at the beginning of the 20th century, presumably because of the work of such organisations. In 1901 the parish registers show that out of eight deaths, only one was an infant.

MEDICAL FACILITIES IN THE 20TH CENTURY

Although a surgeon had been listed in the 1841 census, in the early part of the 20th century there was no doctor in the village. The nearest were either Dr Todd at Marton or Dr Abrahams at Wolston and a visit to the surgeries required a lengthy walk. Cost was also a factor and goods, such as eggs or rabbits, were sometimes used to pay the doctor's bill.

"Between 1897 and 1913 Jane Kaysbrook, wife of Daniel Parrott, kept a diary of all deaths and marriages. It records villagers who survived into their eighties and nineties."

Eventually a district nurse was allocated to the village and she would usually be called before the doctor to reduce the cost. Almost all babies were born at home with the nurse in attendance.

Epidemics continued to take their toll: Not long after the 1914-18 war, Asian flu plagued the country. More people died in the district from the disease than were killed in the war, including the doctor and policeman in Wolston.

The first medical service in the village came with the establishment of a part-time weekly clinic in the Village Hall. In 1951 Dr McElwain applied for surgery facilities in the annex; the request was granted at a cost of 5 shillings for 3 half hour sessions per week.

He later set up a permanent surgery with pharmacy facilities at the side of his home in School Lane. This continued after his death, under several general practitioners: Dr Rees, Dr Menon, Dr Gallagher and Dr Edmonds until Dr Houghton moved the surgery to purpose-built premises in Brookside in the mid 1980s.

Dr Houghton has been joined by a partner, Dr Kay Bridgeman. The modern surgery was extended further in the late 1990s and now provides a full range of services, including ante-natal, mother & baby and 'well-woman' clinics. A practice manager, dispenser, and practice nurse all operate at the surgery and there are a number of associated staff, including a health visitor and midwife.

"There was never any rubbish in the Brook - people depended on it."

Mr Ring outside his cottage in Well Head.

WATER SUPPLY

The water supply to the village had always been plentiful, mainly from the spring at the north corner of the Fosse Way and Brookside. Much of this water was collected

> "Monday was washday and tubs were filled from the brook before being taken to the wash-house at the rear of each cottage. The copper was filled and the fire lit underneath before adding the clothes for a hot wash."

at the Well Head by the Five Acre footpath in Brookside, where the water was so clean that water cress was plentifully grown and sold by the inhabitants of the cottages nearby.

Many other wells were sunk and pumps set up to provide drinking water. For laundry purposes some houses collected rainwater in tanks or simply washed clothes at the side of the brook.

FROM THE 1930's

> "Mrs Burton from the cottages behind the post office did the laying out when people died. She was also a sort of amateur midwife and did the washing when a new baby was born. Mothers were confined to bed for longer then."

In the late 1920s the owners of the Manor House and The Knob arranged to have water piped to their houses from the Well Head by means of an engine pump and iron pipes. Some of the old pipes can still be seen by the electricity transformer near the Fosse Way. An underground water tank was also found under the village green in the 1960s which was presumably part of this system. Most villagers, however, had to wait until the 1930s for such luxury when the Coventry Water Undertaking Corporation installed a piped supply from a mains pipe on the London Road.

> "The brook was still extremely important and was kept very clean. The women fetched water for washing at "Lady Holes" (also known as "Laden Holes") and it was also used to fill up the steam engines for threshing."

SEWAGE DISPOSAL

Until the mid 20th century, toilets had often been at the bottom of the garden in a shed containing a bucket, although the more fortunate may have had some form of commode. The waste was covered with ashes or soil and the contents either thrown onto the garden or collected for fertiliser by a local farmer or gardener.

> "In the 1920s, ladies often used to gather along the railings by the brook to gossip. One Sunday evening a loud crack and splashes were heard as the railings gave way, depositing ladies in their church finery into the water. They were hauled out and dried off to gales of laughter from the nearby cottages."

In 1936 sewer pipes were installed which took both storm and foul water from the houses to a large tank near the Shoulder of Mutton. Once the solid waste had settled, this was extracted with "an unusual wooden scoop" by the collector, Jack Newton, for dispersal on local fields. The liquid from the waste simply trickled into the Brook. A more suitable system was installed in 1961 which separated the foul waste from the storm water using different pipes. This was then pumped from a pumping station in the meadows to a treatment plant at Wolston.

"I remember when a local dustman was fortunate enough to find a discarded jacket on his rounds. While standing in "The Oak" one evening, he pulled out a bundle of unpaid bills from the pocket which were immediately identified by the man standing next to him. Needless to say, the bills were returned but not the jacket!"

There was little household rubbish which needed special disposal. Recycling, mending and "making do" was a way of life until the more affluent 1960s. Edible waste was collected for animal feed and the rag and bone men would collect items which could be reused. General domestic rubbish was also collected in pits. Maps of Stretton prior to the 20th century show a number of these around the village. In the 1980s a Victorian tip in Frankton Lane revealed a quantity of old medicine bottles.

"All my mother longed for was a plumbed-in toilet."

Up until recent times the village had a road sweeper. The centre of the village and up the lanes was kept very clean and tidy. The sweeper's duties also extended to keeping the hedges clipped, cutting the verges with a scythe and even cleaning out the drains.

POWER

Electricity was introduced into the village in the early 1930s, bringing a more convenient way of cooking and lighting than the coal stoves and oil lamps used in the previous century. With no street lighting, however, the streets remained dark but following a fatality when a cyclist from Wolston was killed after colliding with pedestrians who were leaving the Village Hall, the residents pressed for street lighting. White light bulb lamps and posts were erected at irregular points around the village.

"In 1901, a 32 year old man was killed in Knob Hill by lightening in an electric storm which also killed a horse and injured seven other people in the village."

In the early 1970s the Parish Council arranged for the installation of more lighting. These were sodium lamps which gave an orange glow, causing considerable disagreement amongst the residents. In 1999 plans are underway to replace this system with new lighting.

Although solid fuel continued to be used throughout the 20th century, oil central heating was installed by many villagers in the 1960s. It was not until the early 1990s that gas pipes were laid for heating and cooking.

THE FIRE STATION

Some time after the demolition of three cottages at the rear of the Shoulder of Mutton, a brick and wooden building was constructed to house a unit of the National Fire Service during the Second World War. This was manned by local volunteers every evening throughout the war and was fully equipped with helmets, gas masks and fire fighting devices. Two tanks were installed under the village green to supply water in an emergency. In the 1950s the building was sold to the pub by the Ministry of Defence for use as a chicken hut.

Stretton Fire Brigade of 1911.

These cottages, no longer standing, were at the bottom of Church Hill, opposite the Village Hall.

6

A CARING COMMUNITY
HARD TIMES AND CHARITABLE TRUSTS

From medieval times until the 18th century, the prosperity of the inhabitants of any village depended largely on the way it was governed. The early settlements would mainly have been controlled by the lords of the manor and the church, as described in earlier chapters. The parish as a unit of government only emerged as significant in the 15th and 16th century at the same time as the importance of the manor declined.

THE POOR LAWS

The introduction of the first Poor Law of 1563 gave the parish a new role. Under the new law, every parish was required to be responsible for the relief of its own poor. To prevent the migration of the poor to richer communities, no-one could leave their parish unless the parish provided a 'testimonial' of their continued responsibility. No-one legally became an inhabitant until they had lived in a parish for 12 months and once this status was achieved, the parish would be obliged to provide poor relief. The overseers of parishes, who were anxious to keep the village resources for their own people, frequently expelled a pauper who had arrived from elsewhere. The records for Stretton list several examples of paupers attempting to gain settlement in the village and being returned to their original parishes. In one of many examples, Robert Eyre was charged in 1635 with receiving and harbouring paupers. Another cites a relative of a local man being returned to his own parish.

This often caused ill feeling between individual parishes. In the Quarter Sessions records for 1653, William Corrall and wife, who had attempted to settle in Stretton, were returned to Pailton. In the next quarter, Pailton parish disputed this and tried to return them to Stretton.

PARISH REGISTERS OF DEATHS ALSO PROVIDED INSIGHTS INTO THE HAZARDS OF LIFE FOR THOSE WHO WERE POOR:	
1696	"A child found in ye parish of Stretton and buried at Stretton September 15th"
1724	"was baptised Elizabeth Chance a child left upon the town of Princethorpe"
1724	"was buried an unknown person, a woman"
1727	"was buried Frances Smith who was accidentally drowned in a well at Mr Noye's Groat House in Stretton"
1729	"was buried a beggar boy unknown"
1748	"Buried the child of a stranger", "Buried a stranger pauper", "Buried a stranger from Knightlow Hill, "Buried a stranger from the Black Dog"

A further parish responsibility was that of housing. In the 17th century no new cottage was to be erected without a minimum amount of land sufficient to support a family.

The obligations of the parish were often made lighter by the charitable donations and trusts which were available locally. In Stretton such charities were of considerable significance.

Stretton charities

For at least 400 hundred years and probably much longer, some of the land within Stretton has been set aside for the benefit of the poor. The origins of these 'charity lands' are not clear but they still exist today and their income continues to be used for various deserving causes.

There are three such parcels of land. The first is known as the Church and Poor's Land and is made up of several fields at Denchwood, on the north side of the London Road. The second is called the Poor's Plot from which Plott Lane derives its name and is dealt with later in the chapter. The third is a field known as Stretton Close or Field which is situated on the east side of the Fosse Way just before the boundary with Princethorpe.

In 1656 the case is recorded of Mary Church of Stretton whose house was said to be too small for her to inhabit with her four children. The lord of the manor was then required "to allot unto her some small parcel of ground that she may enlarge her house thereon."

The records do not tell us how, when or by whom this land was first set aside, although it is recorded that the Poor's Plot was allocated in return for other strips of land when the village was enclosed in 1704. Stretton Close was allocated under the 1762 Act of Parliament which enclosed Princethorpe.

Bequests from 17th and 18th centuries

The Stretton Charities, as they are collectively known today, are not only allocations of land from the long-distant past. They also include a number of charitable bequests made by benefactors during the 17th and 18th centuries. In most cases, their wishes were quite explicit, as you can see from the following extracts.

The first, Mary Turner, who actually lived in Ryton, left property in 1607 to provide an annual payment of £3 6s 8d to be divided among the neighbouring villages 'towards the relief of the poor impotent and most needy people being not unthrifty nor lusty lazy persons.' Stretton's share was 6s 8d.

In 1687, Elizabeth Taylor willed that from the income from her land in Stretton and Princethorpe, a payment of £3 every seventh year should be applied towards 'putting out an apprentice.' She also left 13s 4d 'for the yearly preaching of two sermons, one upon New Year's day and the other on the Monday of Easter week.'

Her example was followed by her brother, William Herbert, who in 1694 bequeathed all of his property in Shilton to provide from the rents and profits, 40 shillings yearly for life to each of 'three aged men and three aged widows of the town of Stretton-upon-Dunsmore, if such should be there found, or else to six such other persons as should have most need.'

Like his sister, William was also concerned with spiritual matters and left a 20 shillings provision to the minister for the yearly preaching of two sermons at Stretton church, one on Ascension Day and the other on 21st October. But his overriding concern for people was illustrated by his third bequest which was to fund the apprenticing of one poor boy or girl 'to some good trade' every two years.

Stretton also benefited from the 1711 will of a Bilton man, William Smith, which provided 4s each year to a number of parishes in the area 'to be distributed in bread to the poorest people.'

In 1719 another benefactor, Henry Johnson, charged that his 'lands and tenements' in Stretton-on-Dunsmore should provide 10s a year 'to be distributed in bread by the churchwardens and overseers to the poor of the parish on the Sunday next before Twelfth Day.'

The last bequest was made by Rhoda Marriott in 1827 who left the interest from a £10 savings account 'to be expended in bread on every New Year's day and given to such aged poor widows and widowers of this parish who should have attended divine service on that day.'

LATER ADDITIONS AND CHANGES TO THE CHARITIES PROPERTY

In addition to the original cottages and outbuildings at Shilton left by William Herbert, the Charities owned a number of cottages in Stretton which had been erected on their lands (probably during the late 18th or early 19th century). These were rented out by the Trustees and the income used to supplement the benefits.

In 1831 these properties were described as 'a cottage with garden and part of thatched building formerly a dairy, ...another cottage situated on the south side of the road to the church, ...a new brick-built cottage and garden on south side of high road, ...a cottage and garden held by Mary Clarke, a very aged person, for her life... and a building lately erected at the Poor's Plot on south side of lane to Oxford Road.'

Today only a pair of houses in Brookside which had formerly been the original school and school house, together with two in Shilton, remain owned by the Charities. The funds raised by the sale of property have been invested in equities and continue to provide income to the Charities.

EARLY ADMINISTRATION OF THE CHARITIES' FUNDS

Before the 17th century, it is uncertain how the income from the Poor's Plot and the Church and Poor's land was actually distributed to the poor. We must presume that it was administered by the churchwardens as they themselves were entitled to receive some of this income for the upkeep of the church: a right which is maintained to this day.

By the 18th century, the Poor's Plot and the Church and Poor's Land had been effectively combined for administrative purposes. In the first part of the 19th century, it had become the custom for this income, together with the Stretton Close rent, to be given out in coal to the poor each St. John's Day (27 December).

Where income had come from wills, the executors and their families ensured that the wishes of the deceased were put into effect. For example the records show that in the 1830's Thomas Johnson, presumably a descendant of Henry Johnson, purchased 10s worth of bread for distribution to the poor as directed by the original will of 1719. However, the control of these individual charities eventually passed to various separate sets of trustees.

SUPPORT OF EDUCATION ADDED TO THE AIMS OF THE CHARITIES

In the late 18th century, it appears that through economic necessity, parents would rather their children worked for wages than be unpaid apprentices. At the same time, there was a growing appreciation nationally of the importance of education and free schools were being established in many areas.

As so few of Stretton's poor were willing to have their children apprenticed, the trustees and parishioners decided that a village school would be more beneficial. Since rents from the Charities' lands in Shilton had doubled to £30 a year since the enclosure, funds were available for setting up a free school and in 1786 a case was put to the Attorney General, Sir Pepper Arden, asking him to confirm that this would be 'consonant with the will of the donor.' Sir Pepper agreed and the first village school was set up in what are now numbers 64 & 66 Brookside. Detail of how the school developed is covered in Chapter 7.

FURTHER SUPPORT FOR EDUCATION IN 1859

The church appeared to have had much influence in the overall administration of the village charities. In the 1850s, the vicar promoted a new scheme to combine the management of the Poor's Plot, Poor & Church Lands and the Herbert charities. A draft scheme was put to the Charities Commission. The choice of the trustees for this new, improved scheme was not without some difference of opinion. Three local farmers objected so strongly to the Vicar's proposed list of trustees that they petitioned the Charity Commissioners. Their complaint centred around the 'preponderance of clergy over laity' and in particular they objected to the Reverend Randolph Skipwith because he was a non-resident and the Reverend C Blencowe Shuckburgh because of his 'greatly advanced years.' Their petition must have succeeded as neither of these two clerics were listed as trustees when the scheme was finally approved in 1859.

THE 1859 SCHEME

The Scheme combined the Poor's Plot, Herbert and the Church & Poor's Lands Charities under one set of trustees. From the income of the Herbert Charity, the following original terms of his will were confirmed:

The traditional payment of one half of the income from the Church and Poor's Land to the Churchwardens towards the repairs of the Parish Church was continued.

A school was to be maintained from the remaining income of these charities, including accommodation for the Master and Mistress. The result was the building of a school at the corner of Plott Lane and Dog Lane (now School Lane).

Any income outstanding was to assist the sick and support coal or clothing clubs. A statement from the charities dated 1852 also mentions the provision of 'soup at a reduced cost in winter.'

THE COAL AND CLOTHING CLUBS

The 1859 Scheme restructured the original provisions for the needy from the Poor's Plot and Church & Poor's Lands. Poor people who were sick were helped on an individual basis but other arrangements were formalised through the creation of The Coal Club and The Clothing Club. Instead of donations being made directly to individuals, it allowed the trustees to make annual payments of up to £25 to a village coal club, £16 to a clothing club and £25 towards caring for the sick.

> The 1880 rules of the Clothing Club included this severe warning;
>
> 'Drunkenness, dishonesty, or any profligacy of any kind, or neglect of children's education shall disqualify a Member for any addition to his or her deposit for the year.'

Each of the two clubs had rules governing eligibility and kept their own accounts. 'Poor people of good character' could join the Coal Club but the Clothing Club was originally limited to 'the labouring class only.'

Those eligible paid a monthly subscription. At the end of the year, the sum saved plus the member's share of the charities' contribution that year was returned in the form of coals or clothing vouchers.

Both Clubs expected certain standards from their Members. In the case of Coal, any difficulty regarding the character or eligibility of members or applicants was referred to the Trustees for a final decision.

The Clubs continued for many years but as the level of financial hardship in the village reduced, fewer people were eligible for membership and numbers gradually declined. Both were finally wound up in the early 1970s.

FURTHER CHANGES TO ADMINISTRATION

The 'bread' charities (Johnson & Marriott) benefited many villagers over a very long period. Even as late as 1915, over one hundred loaves were being handed out annually in accordance with the wishes of the benefactors. At the end of the First World War, the Trustees of the Johnson and Marriott charities recognised that the bread distributions were no longer appropriate. They obtained authorisation to use the funds for 'clothing, linen, bedding, fuel, tools, medical care and food for the poor.' Similarly, it was agreed that if the apprenticeship grant was not used under the Taylor charity, this could be applied to under 21 year olds to assist them in preparing for an occupation.

BENEFICIARIES

It is difficult to identify the very many village people who have benefited over the centuries but there are notable exceptions. For example, William Herbert actually selected six of the first recipients of his £4 annuity by naming them in his 1694 will.

In the past, when there were no pension schemes, these payments had great significance. However, for payment to continue the trustees expected certain standards of behaviour to be maintained.

Those who benefited were known as 'annuitants' and this term has continued to the present day when small payments are made annually to a number of our senior citizens.

In the early years, the 'setting out' of apprentices certainly occurred as the benefactors had intended and the practice continued regularly at least until the 1840's with instances of this type of assistance being recorded up until the end of the century. However, these payments were only occasionally requested and as early as the 1790's demand was so low that the trustees began to explore other ways of helping young people.

> ### THE FIRST ANNUITANTS NAMED IN WILLIAM HERBERT'S 1694 WILL
>
> *William Boddington,*
> *John Constance (the elder)*
> *and his wife Joane,*
> *John Browne,*
> *William Satchwell*
> *and Widow Shyers.*

THE CHARITIES TODAY

By 1962, the administration of all the charities had been transferred to the Trustees of the 1859 Scheme. Today, the administration of all of the individual charities is undertaken by one board of eight trustees. The land and property owned by the Charities are managed by the Trustees and the revenues are broadly used for the same purposes as set out in the 1859 scheme. The Trust continues to provide significant support to the education and training of our children but it is worth noting that,

> " *In the minute book for 1825, it is noted that John Lansdale was struck off from the list of aged 'having forfeited his character for sobriety' and in 1846 Widow Jane White, who was no longer resident in village, was given an ultimatum that unless she returned by 1 May, she would be succeeded by the Widow Lansdale*".

despite the many changes to the various provisions since the 18th century, William Herbert's 1694 annuities to 'three aged men and three aged widows of the town of Stretton-upon-Dunsmore' are still being paid to this very day.

THE PLOTT

For well over two hundred years there was a distinct community within the village living on the Poor's Plot referred to earlier. At one time there were some 130 people living in cottages either side of Plott Lane and partly supported by allotments created for their use. Of this community virtually nothing now remains. "Plott Cottage" represents the last of the original buildings, although the surrounding allotment land is still largely in use.

Although the first documentary reference to this community is in the enclosure settlement of 1704 (see Chapter 2), there appear to have been poor people living in this area before then. A pre-enclosure map of the village refers to "The Poors" living at the top of what we now know as Plott Lane. When and why they came to be there is not known - perhaps the enclosure arrangements produced a formal allocation of land to 'squatters' who already lived at the edge of the village. In the enclosure settlement a 'plot' was allocated for the poor of Stretton on either side of the 'Coventry Way.' The 'plott' became known as 'The Poor Land' or the 'Poor Plott' and, in turn, the lane itself became known as 'Plott Lane.'

The land is listed in 'The Quality Book' of 1821 as "Poor Close, the Slang and two closes next to the turnpike road" (which was the London Road). The name 'Slang' is still used by villagers today to describe the long thin strips on either side of the lane, near the modern playing field. Although now overgrown, these strips were narrow allotments which were still in use within living memory (for example, for keeping pigs in the 1940s and 50s). The line of some can be traced in the area around the old Methodist Chapel. A little further up the lane, two allotments still survive intact on the south side. The more extensive land for the poor, however, was found in the fields bounded by Plott Lane and Freeboard Lane. This is still

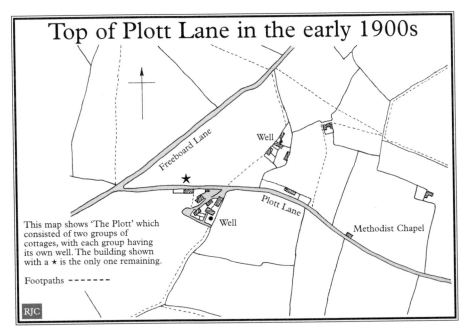

Top of Plott Lane in the early 1900s

Freeboard Lane

Well

★

Plott Lane

Well

Methodist Chapel

This map shows 'The Plott' which consisted of two groups of cottages, with each group having its own well. The building shown with a ★ is the only one remaining.

Footpaths - - - - - - -

RJC

One of the now demolished cottages at 'The Plott'.

owned and let by the Parish and by Stretton Charities.

By the 19th century, the settlement was quite substantial and further land was also being added. An indenture at the County Records Office records the purchase of land in 1853 by the Churchwardens and overseers of the poor who paid £32 "of lawful British money" to buy land "for the benefit of the Poor Inhabitants of the parish." By the 20th century there were nineteen cottages, although at one time there may have been more.

The cottages were found in three clusters. The largest group, known as "The Close", was on the south side of the lane and included the present Plott Cottage (which was in fact made up of two cottages). The others were set further back and approached through what is now the entrance to allotments. On the north side of the land four terraced cottages stood on the site of the present bungalow and another terrace further into the present allotments. This was called "Robinson's Close" after one of the families living there.

> *"It was nice to up there in summer" but with walls of single brick thickness, winter was a difficult time. The pond behind Plott Cottage also served as a source of water and one former resident recalls his grandfather shaving in it each morning.*
> *One of the cottages seemed to have served as a small shop selling groceries and Mr Nix was noted for his ginger wine; unfortunately this was non-alcoholic and drinkers had to seek such comfort in the village inns.*

The census returns for 1861 show a community of over 130 people. By 1891 this had fallen to just under 90. Even at the end of the century, three quarters of the community had been born in Stretton. The men were invariably agricultural labourers and nearly twenty women and children were listed as silk winders. This is borne out by a record of around 1830 showing a new building at the Poor's Plot being let by the trustees to the churchwarden and overseer for the poor, on the condition that it was used to employ poor children. This employment is thought to have been silk winding or 'gimping.'

What was life at the Plott like? Although it was a distinct community, it was also part of the village. There was considerable continuity in the families living there, with the same names recurring in the records well into the 20th century. The cottages were typical for the area: red brick and thatched (some were later given galvanised roofs). Many had just one downstairs room, with perhaps a small kitchen or pantry at the back.

The only house which remains of the community known as 'The Plott'.

There were no 'mod cons' and the privy was usually at the bottom of the garden and often shared. Water came from two nearby pumps, one of which can still be seen at the side of Plott Lane.

The adjacent allotments provided vegetables and fruit, some of which might be sold and, in more than one case, pushed on a hand cart to market. The larger 'pieces' were big enough for growing wheat and barley for animal feed. The small brick building next to Plott Cottage served as a threshing shed. As elsewhere in the village, pigs and poultry were an essential part of the family diet.

Work on the allotments was not allowed on Sundays, probably because there was a strong link between the people at the Plott and the Primitive Methodist chapel (see Chapter 3).

The community at the Plott declined rapidly after the Second World War. The houses were in an increasingly poor state and once abandoned, they were demolished. The absence of proper foundations meant that the land was easily turned over to the allotments we know today. Some inhabitants found temporary accommodation in the former camp at the bottom of the Lane and many more moved to new housing built in the village in the 1950s. By the mid 1950s only a handful of people remained of the original community.

THE FRIENDLY SOCIETY

By the end of the 18th century a large number of "friendly societies" had been established throughout the country. These had numerous functions but mainly offered a form of inexpensive insurance against illness. On 1 January 1776 a 'Friendly Society' was established at 'The Black Dog' public house on the London Road. Meetings were later held at the Shoulder of Mutton. The subscriptions collected by the Friendly

Society were paid out to villagers in times of sickness or as funeral expenses.

After twelve months of membership, members would become eligible for benefit. Should they fall ill, they would be visited by the Stewards of the society and paid a sum appropriate to length of membership but starting at three shillings a week.

A feast day was held every year on Whit Monday at the Shoulder of Mutton which included a procession, festive fare and entertainment but even on such a day, rules were tightly applied: should any member be seen to give bread, meat or beer away, they would forfeit two shillings and sixpence; any member not answering their name at roll call but in health and living within a certain distance would be fined or excluded.

> *"A surviving copy of the Rules and Orders of the society dated 1861 indicates that meetings were run on very strict lines. Members would forfeit two shillings if they disputed a decision, officers of the committee could be fined one shilling for neglect of duty and even the publican was obliged to forfeit the same if he allowed anyone other than a member into a meeting".*

> *"A close watch was clearly kept for any malingering: anyone found "gaming, fishing or doing work for lucre or gain or being more than one mile from his residence, except for going to Church" would be fined or excluded. In fact, such was the sternness of the book of rules that a forfeit was applied to those who failed to inform on those who claimed benefit falsely".*

It is not clear whether such severe restrictions continued into the 20th century but modern memories confirm that if a villager was receiving payment for illness, they were not allowed out of their homes after 9 o'clock in the evening and that "members of the society would go round and visit anyone claiming to be ill. If they were not at home, they would lose their benefit." One incident of a Friendly Society 'malingerer' is recalled of a lady seen fetching water and reported as fit to carry the bucket.

THE SICK AND DIVIDEND SOCIETY

The Oak and Black Dog also ran a similar society although this is thought to have started much later.

Whatever the restrictions of these arrangements, there is no doubt that such societies provided an important means of support during hard times. The Sick and Dividend Society remained in operation until the 1950s.

> *"I can remember the Oak & Black Dog 'Sick and Dividend Society.'*
> *This was before the Second World War. My father was the secretary of it*
> *and every Sunday afternoon, it was my job to go round and deliver the*
> *money to people who were sick. They received 10 shillings a week. This was*
> *the only means of support they had but, in those days, 10 shillings was*
> *quite a lot of money (1935).*
> *They paid out a dividend at Christmas and people relied on this to buy*
> *their presents."*

THE WORKHOUSE

Although the village organisations provided reasonable assistance to the poor, some still became destitute. Workhouses were first set up under the Workhouse Test Act in 1722 to house those who received no other support. Conditions in the workhouses throughout the country were harsh on the general principle that people should be discouraged from becoming totally dependent on charity. Men and women were kept apart in dormitories, given a variety of labouring work to do and sufficient food to prevent starvation. In the 18th century, local property owners were required to pay a poor rate to the Rugby Workhouse Union. Fixed contributions from Stretton to the 'indoor poor' maintained those people who were from the village. Other recipients were 'outdoor poor' who lived at home but received supplementary income from the Union. In 1852 this was 9s 9d per week (about 48 pence). Stretton recorded nine people who were ill, infirm, orphaned or deserted.

> *"In 1859 six Stretton people, including an entire family, had been sent to the Rugby workhouse".*

The 20th century brought the closure of the workhouses and the introduction of the welfare state system which we know today.

*Two views of the same cottage in Brookside,
now sadly missing from the village scene.*

7

TEACHING THE YOUNG
HISTORY OF THE SCHOOL

THE FIRST SCHOOL IN STRETTON

The first school in Stretton was an example of the privately endowed Charity Schools, which in the late 17th and 18th centuries provided elementary education for the poor. Several charities for poor children and aged poor men and women from Stretton were established mostly under the will of William Herbert, dated August 15, 1694 (see Chapter 6). These charities did not specifically include a school but by the latter half of the 18th century the Trustees and parishioners decided it would be beneficial to erect a free school from the endowment to instruct a certain number of poor boys and girls of the Parish. A mistress was to be appointed with a yearly stipend of £10 10s and use of a school house.

The Rev William Daniel, Vicar of the Parish, duly begged a piece of ground from the Trustees, which had been conveyed for that purpose by a Mrs Smith, and a school house was erected in Brookside by subscriptions from the parishioners and the Vicar. The school opened on Lady Day 1789 under the charge of a school mistress Miss Mary Mason.

To endow a charity school such as this was common in the 18th century. No other form of elementary education was generally available and most children of the poor had no expectation of education at all unless from charities endowed by a benefactor. However, charitable education was primarily intended to benefit poor children in such a way that they would understand their duty towards God and become useful labourers and servants. There was strong demand that the instruction given should be rudimentary and of a practical and industrial kind. This was reflected in the proposed curriculum for the Stretton School which required that the children should be taught to read, sew, knit and spin. Reading was considered necessary to enable them to read the Bible and Catechism and provide religious and moral instruction.

Stretton's original school house is now numbers 64 and 66 Brookside.

By 1810 school records show that the school at Brookside taught 24 girls and 12 boys of the Church of England.

THE NATIONAL SCHOOL

By the mid 19th century education was no longer regarded as a charity to be given to the poor and attempts were underway to establish a satisfactory national system of education. As a result, like many other charity schools, Stretton School became a "national" school.

The Committee of the Council on Education determined in what manner the grants of money made from time to time by Parliament should be distributed. This committee collected information from the grant-aided schools and began building up a policy of educational advancement and also established the "pupil teacher" system. It did not control school management but exercised supervision of all grant-aided schools under the management of voluntary bodies. In the case of Church schools, which included Stretton, the vicar of the Parish was usually the chairman of the managers and was given the right to use the premises as a Sunday School. The vicar of Stretton performed this function and several of the Trustees of the Herbert Charities acted as school managers.

POOR CONDITIONS

At the outset, most National Schools were free, though some made a charge of a penny a week. In 1862 the school fee at Stretton was 1½ d a week, ½ d of which was for copybooks. However, the new controls did not immediately improve conditions and Her Majesty's Inspectors' Report described conditions at the school building that year as follows:

"The present schoolrooms are low, ill-ventilated and inconveniently arranged. The master deserves high praise for his hard work....My Lords trust that the managers will take immediate steps to provide better premises. Their Lordships will scarcely feel warranted in paying further annual grants to the school in its present state."

Stretton's second school was built in 1861 and stood at the junction of School Lane and Plott Lane.

In fact, although the move to new premises in School Lane was achieved in time for the next annual inspection, 'My Lords' still did not feel warranted to pay further grants.

THE SCHOOL LOGBOOK

In 1861 a new schoolmaster, Mr Leech, had been appointed at an annual salary of £60. The new education system appeared to have had little effect on him and records show him continuing with his work much as he had done before. He noted an improvement in writing, was manifestly pleased with an illustrated lesson on history, questioned the boys on grammar and scripture and observed, *"Good day's work: prosecution of arithmetic with success."* In the next six months he referred to the teaching of music, learning the Gospel of St Mark and tackling 'the rule of three in vulgar fractions.' 'Decency' was also encouraged.

On October 1 1862 Mr Leech began a logbook which was to be continued by successive headmasters. Although the first entry: *"Allowed boys to play 40 mins in pm. Corrected boy for accidentally breaking slate"* is blunt and practical, the log book provides an insight into school life over the years.

Girls were taught by an uncertified mistress in an adjoining part of the building. Boys were sometimes sent home to wash and comb or get clean pinafores and were sometimes recorded as disorderly. There are also references to boys at Night School, who appear to have received the same kind of instruction.

Irregularity of attendance at school, a national problem, was felt keenly by the Victorian masters at Stretton School. Apart from the demands of home and the nearby farmers, which were strong and traditional, there was a silk mill at Brandon which employed child labour. In addition to his 40 or so boys, Mr Leech also noted that occasional 'working boys' or 'factory boys' came or were sent to his school.

Several times the master noted that gimping (a cottage industry of twisting silk for trimmings) interfered with progress and other problems were caused by the local hunt, the wedding of the Royal Prince, playing truant to go bird nesting or mothers taking their boys to spend the Clothing Club money at Coventry. He admits to 'depression on account of parental indifference.'

FROM TIME TO TIME, THERE IS NOTE OF SADNESS IN THE SCHOOLMASTER'S ENTRIES DURING THE YEAR:

"Great discouragement from the indifferences of parents in sending their children to school."
and frequent evidence of children being kept from school
for economic reasons:
"Gathering acorns, fetching pair of boots, wheat setting, bean setting, plough driving."

RURAL LIFE GAVE MANY REASONS FOR ABSENTEEISM IN THE 19TH CENTURY			
Wells, 13	Gimping	**Lydiatt**, 12	Getting potatoes
Barnwell, 10	Minding the toll gate	**Washbrooke**, 8	Scruffling
Manton, 11	Driving plough	**Dumbleton**, 8	Setting Barley
Haynes, 11	Minding the toll gate	**Baylis**, 9	Setting Oats
Terry, 12	Oat setting	**Berry**, 9	Stone picking
Mawley, 11	Sheep tending	**Osborne**, 6	Gimping
Hobday, 9	Want of money	**Smith**, 7	Clothes to be
Humphreys, 6	Clothes torn through bird nesting		washed or repaired

An extract from the school log shows the ages of the pupils.

THE DEVELOPING SCHOOL

At the end of 1862, Her Majesty's Inspection was held. There is only a brief record of the result but several points are of interest:

That year the Inspectors decided that, because the endowment of the boys' school yielded more than 30 shillings a year for every scholar according to the average number in attendance, the grant would be withheld. No grant was due to the girls' school as it was not in the charge of a "certificated" teacher. The grant to the Night School was also withheld for the same reason.

Boys :	Discipline fair. Religious knowledge fair. Knowledge of secular subjects moderate.
Girls :	Buildings new and good. Discipline pretty good. Instruction moderate. Religious knowledge pretty fair, a few answered nicely. Six night scholars attended, of whom four had been present 24 nights. All passed in reading and 2 in arithmetic.
	All failed in dictation.

However, thanks to his relation with the Charities and his relation with the managers (with money at their disposal), the schoolmaster at Stretton was in a safer position than in a non-endowed school which would be dependant on Government grants and subject to children's attendance and examination results. Even so, the resources of the charity did not rise with the increasing cost of education and Stretton School was to feel financial pressure in later years.

The new controls also laid down that the girls must receive instruction in plain needlework. However, the logbook rarely refers to the girls or the schoolmistress, except to record the punishment of a boy for trespassing on the girls' premises.

The discipline which Mr Leech felt necessary did not come easily to him and he was not happy about the sharp hits he sometimes had to give. He lists examples of punishing boys for scrumping apples in the Pool Yard and for putting spiders into ale barrels. In fact the Vicar chided him for lenience and muddled him still more.

The Vicar was a frequent visitor to the School. He read prayers or examined the boys in arithmetic. On one occasion, the master wrote: "Vicar in playground, progress in school." It also seemed that, even in the 19th century, not only the vicar but the increasing demands for results placed the headmaster under considerable pressure. In the same year he wrote his last entry: "Thus ends my record..... John Henry Leech, Schoolmaster." He had found less burdensome employment with the Cambridge Press Library.

His successor, Mr Walker, was a trained teacher, straight from College. A certificate from the Privy Council Office stated : *"Robert Walker is a good teacher, fluent and animated. His lesson was well arranged, well illustrated and interesting. As a schoolmaster he is patient, persevering and successful."*

He quickly brought the syllabus up to date by introducing notation. He also sent boys home to their mothers to collect their missing school fees. However, he was soon dealing with the old problem of indifference and he noted philosophically: *"The poorer classes will not deny themselves for the sake of their children, nor can we expect them to do so when 10 shillings a week is all they obtain for their labour."*

Despite this, his perseverance is shown in such entries as this one after an arithmetic lesson: *"took Standard 4 again through all the rules."* He ordered new reading books. He admitted 'little boys' to school and expressed his concern that there was no infant school in Stretton. The Inspectors' reports reflected their impression of his efficiency and recommended the reorganising of the school as a mixed school so that the 'cider girls' might have the benefit of his teaching arithmetic (although there is no explanation of 'cider girls'). The Assistant Mistress, who came with Mr Leech from the old school, looked after the girls and eventually the Infant School.

Mr Walker stayed eight years - long enough to see Stretton School achieve its first Annual Grant for ten years.

Stretton school at the turn of the century.

57

THE EFFECTS OF THE 1870 EDUCATION ACT

It was Mr W J Hassall who was to experience the effect of the 1870 Education Act in Stretton.

In 1870 W E Forster, Vice-President of the Education Department, brought in his historic Education Act. This allowed Voluntary Schools (in the care of religious bodies) to continue their work alongside the newly authorised 'Board' schools.

With a less strict approach to religious instruction incorporated into the Act, many schools now discontinued the practice of attending church services. However in May 1871, the logbook records that in Stretton *'the boys and girls went to Church on Ascension Day as usual.'*

The Act also required parents with children of not less than 5 years and not more than 13 years to send them to school, although provisions for exemption were made for children between 10 and 13 years who had reached a certain standard. Unless a child was receiving other education or was sick or lived three miles from school, he was legally obliged to attend.

> *"The plan of dividing the school into numerous groups seems to answer well, and every child seems to be more interested than when they had to wait for turns so long in a large class."*
>
> *"Am afraid that the Infants learn to repeat the additional tables from the answers going in numerical order, which is not effort on the mind but really of rote."*

MR HASSALL'S RECORDS

When Mr Hassall began teaching at Stretton as a young man, he had approximately 35 children on his register. There were also about 24 in the infant School. This figure does not materially change for another ten years.

Mr Hassall with schoolmistress and pupils at the turn of the century.

From time to time the new master noted traditional absences but almost all the entries are about his job and the boys he taught.

The following extracts from the log give us some idea of his methods:

In 1874 needlework appeared in the subjects qualifying for a grant and Mr Hassall introduced French exercises. He also took the trouble to go into the playground to teach the children games: *"Taught the children games - Birds in a cage, Cats and Mice, Links in the chain. Set the girls off; they seem to have no heart to start a game themselves but stand around shivering."*

Problems with half-time scholars arose around this time. In June 1875 we learn that some of the children, who were able to attend as "half-timers", and also work, were leaving altogether. Six months later Mr Hassall recorded: *"The half-time boys never come now. I heard this week that some farmers were not sending their boys and those who did have left off sending theirs."*

The schoolmaster also sent a list of the children who travelled from Stretton to Brandon Factory to the Inspector of Factories at Coventry, with a request that the half-timers should attend Stretton not Ryton School. This brought a promise to send "all the Stretton children who work at Brandon to this School next Monday" and "Factory children to the number ten to be returned to school."

Despite such problems, a new relationship was emerging between employers and school. In 1876 Mr Hassall issued his first Labour Certificate as a reference for a school leaver. This was issued at the request of a farmer and read as follows: *"I certify that Frederick Burton attended school an appropriate number of times during the previous 12 months."* The certificate also required the boy to have passed a Standard IV examination in reading, writing and arithmetic.

In 1878, Mr Hassall issued the first Child's School Book for a Stretton school leaver, showing particulars of the child's age and attendance. As many of his pupils are not within sight of Standard 2 pass, he had the task of checking attendances over the past years. Those who did not meet the requirements were awarded a "Dunce's pass."

1880s

"Miss Amy Johnson was the schoolmistress - we called her Polly Ann. We didn't like her much. The boys had to push her in a wheelchair to church and one day they got their own back by letting it go on the hill."

"I hated arithmetic and on the days it was taught, I cried so I could stay at home and look after the baby - for there was always one of those around. But I learnt enough for my needs."

Irregular attendance seemed to result from both sickness and indifference, although Mr Hassall records that many masters in the area were in an even worse plight. In 1879, however, a new system of weekly visits by the School Attendance Officer, Mr Root, improved attendance and brought the school strength up to 100.

As a result of the weekly visits, the first 5 shilling fine on Stretton parents for failing to send their children to school was imposed by Rugby Magistrates in July 1880 (although in 1887 the same family was still in trouble.)

By the end of the 19th century, Labour Certificates were no longer issued by the school but had to be obtained from the School Attendance Office in Rugby. The only parent who actually submitted to this fresh demand was a Mrs Smith, who walked to Rugby and back to appear before the School Attendance Committee, *"although she was not in a fit state to do so."*

During this period the school was staffed solely by the members of the Hassall family and the logbook records the progress of this remarkable family of which five daughters and two sons all became teachers in Warwickshire.

> ## 1915
>
> *"School day started with a prayer and afterwards we learned writing, reading, drawing and poetry. At playtime we played hopscotch and skipping. At lunchtime we would run home, always calling at the farriers to see if a horse was having new shoes."*
>
> *"The headmaster took the examinations and we went up to his desk one at a time. The first paper I did had six sums and I had five wrong and one right. The master said he didn't know how I could have got that right - but I knew I had copied it from a friend!"*
>
> *"Every Sunday morning the vicar would call at the school where we would be in line, ready to march behind him to church. Our summer outings were to Stoneleigh."*

THE SCHOOL IN THE 20TH CENTURY

Before Mr Hassall retired after 36 years, he had seen significant changes. On June 30, 1903 he recorded the last day that the school came under the control of the Trustees of Stretton Charities. On the following day, the school was handed over to the Education Committee of the Warwickshire County Council. The new managers consisted of a member of the County Council, who acted as Chairman, a representative of the Parish Council and four of the old Trustees.

In 1906 the change to perfect copper plate in the log book with the arrival of the new master, Mr Fell, comes as a shock after the shaky script of Mr Hassall's later years. Mr Fell found much to criticise. However, the most interesting notes in the logbook come not in these years but when Mr Fell returned in 1919 after he had served in the First World War.

His first log entry on his return states, "Commenced School Gardening. Have made

> ## 1920's
>
> *"There were as many children living up on the London Road as there were in the village."*
>
> *"Families were a lot larger then and 8 to 12 children was not unusual."*
>
> *"One of our favourite hobbies was making paper boats and following them to see how far they would go. This meant scrambling under the bridges and into the meadows beyond. In those days the water level was much higher and many a child got a good smacking afterwards."*
>
> *"We walked home from school at lunchtime, had a slice of bread and jam and walked back again."*

application to teach rough carpentry, poultry keeping and rabbit keeping." Before long he was requesting the County Agricultural Advisory Committee to consider an application for fruit trees for the school garden.

His achievements were not only in practical subjects. In 1921 he reorganised his top class to work as a private study class and further details are provided by the following extract from the Inspector's report showing how Mr Fell's experiments were being viewed by the Authorities, who reported:

> *"This rural school is of unique interest and value. When the master returned from active service he at once broke away from the old formal routine and developed a curriculum and spirit of work on unusually sound lines of equal attraction to the children and staff. Without special premises or elaborate equipment, he has succeeded in building up a group of practical activities centred round rural life and at the same time he has enlarged the scope and value of the ordinary elementary subjects."*

> *"The children are busy and methodical as bees, and they learn through the compelling interest of their work to combine self-reliance and self-help with offered discipline and corporate action. The boys have a bench and tools in their ordinary classroom. From their sketches and measured drawings they have made all kinds of useful things, utilising old materials where possible, hen coups, egg racks and games apparatus. They take an interest in the history of the village."*

> *"All this handicraft is turned to the best educational use. The pupils: notebooks, well expressed and illustrated. Drawings, balance sheets, inventories of stock, tools, reference books and journeys on rural pursuits all bear witness to the thoroughness of their work. There are no dull children. Each finds his right sphere of interest and looks to the master as friend and counsellor."*

Stretton school class of 1918.

61

1930's

"Behind the old school were the school gardens. When you reached 13, you were given a plot to dig and grow vegetables. We even had about 12 hens and collected eggs. Every year we went on a day trip, sometimes on the train to the seaside or by Mr Quarterman's bus."

Stretton school class photo, 1920-21.

"I lived in Princethorpe and had to walk (and sometimes run) to school in Stretton."

"Caning was allowed."

"We had day trips - sometimes to Wicksteed Park or by train to the seaside."

"Street Games included Whip & top, yo-yo, Tip Cat, 5 Stones, Skipping, Hoops, Hopscotch and Hide & Seek.

"There were no plumbed-in toilets so the four teachers and the pupils used 5 buckets."

Stretton school football team in 1933 with the Headmaster, Mr Austin.

GREATER RESPONSIBILITY

When Mr Fell left in 1924, the new Headmaster, Mr Austin recorded a few glimpses of a different form of development by the local authority, namely the school medical service and allied forms of care. The physical education programme also reflected the growing concern with the health and physical progress of the school child. There was now greater focus on the health of the child and the logbook notes special attention given to the drying of wet clothes. An Act of 1907 had made medical inspection compulsory and by this time the doctor and dentist were calling at the school regularly to examine the children and there were visits from the school nurses and health visitor. Furthermore, if the Inspectors reported problems with the buildings, their recommendations were usually carried out.

School meals were served in the Village Hall. There was a central heating system in the school although the buildings themselves did not yet conform to the required standards in all respects. However, Government grants in 1959 towards improvement to buildings of Aided Schools meant that the Trustees were already considering large scale improvements or even the provision of a new school.

The school continued to provide an excellent education for Stretton children. In the 1930s there was a proud entry recording two boys obtaining special places at Lawrence Sheriff Grammar School, Rugby. By the 1950s village boys and girls were regularly making their mark at local grammar schools and colleges.

1940's

"Classes were divided with screens and there was a stove in the classroom."

"There was wire netting over the windows because of the war and we all had gas masks. At playtime we had bottles of milk which were sometimes frozen solid in winter."

"No-one had school meals or sandwiches. We all went home and mother was always there."

"I had a lovely childhood. After school we would go fishing in the brook or collect armfuls of bluebells and primroses from Bull and Butcher wood."

1950's

"Toys were still simple. After the war years we were interested in all things military. We still made soldiers from melted soup cans. Planes and forts were wooden. We collected things too: stamps, cigarette cards and cheese labels. "We were interested in far off lands."

"The girls made paper dolls and dressed them. At Christmas we all made paper chains."

"The main excitement was from empty orange boxes on old pram wheels which whizzed down Church Hill at great speed, sometimes spilling their occupants into the brook."

"Games were still the same as they had been for centuries - knocking on doors and running away and sometimes tying the handles of adjoining cottage doors together to watch the perplexed faces of the occupants when they emerged."

In January 1956 came the appointment of Mr T A Gullick as headmaster.

"I remember mole-catching which saved gardens from damage but also provided much youthful excitement from skinning and curing the skins!"

"We were allowed to stand by the bus shelter opposite the Oak and watch the hunt meet as part of our lessons."

"There was a big rocking horse in the infant hut."

A NEW DIRECTION

In 1956 Stretton School became a school for children of 5 to 11 years and was renamed Stretton-on-Dunsmore C of E Junior and Infants School. In January 1956 came the appointment of Mr T A Gullick as headmaster.

In September 1973 the old system of an all-through Primary School was changed to First (4-7 years) and Middle (8-12 years), although the Knightlow Church of England First and Middle School was run as a combined school until Marton School closed in December 1973. Children from Marton and also from Ryton joined the school, despite considerable resistance from parents and villagers from the latter. An independent school was established at Ryton but closed by September 1974.

The First School now occupied a new building in Hill Crescent and the new Middle School building on an adjacent site was officially opened on 21 April 1975 by Dr Cuthbert Bardsley, Bishop of Coventry, with Mrs Young (former headteacher of Marton School) as headteacher of the First School and Mr Gullick headteacher of the Middle School. Children no longer attended church services as part of the school curriculum but end of term communion services were started at the Middle School on 15 July 1975.

April 1979 brought several changes: Mrs Young retired and was replaced by Mrs Large and at the same time Mr Hillman was appointed deputy headteacher to replace Mr Booth, who had been in the post since reorganisation. The First School opened that summer term with 83 children on the roll, the Middle School with a roll of 216.

The schools continued to develop. Temporary classrooms were installed and 229 trees were planted in the nature area and around the school. Children enjoyed the benefit of learning music and drama and school trips stretched to more adventurous destinations, including Holland.

In September 1980, Mr Hillman was appointed to the headship, following the retirement of Mr Gullick after 24 years.

1960's

"We used to walk in twos to the Village Hall for school dinners. Mrs Scattergood and Mrs Lewin would be standing 'army fashion', bracing themselves behind a trestle table and would dish up from huge stainless steel containers which had been delivered in a van by Mr Frank Butler from Wolston."

"We had lessons in using the telephone."

"There was no school field. We walked to the Fosse Way Playing Field for sports. These days they would have to lay on a mini bus or they'd be too tired to run in the relay."

A CHANGING SYSTEM

Many adjustments to the education system were to follow. Regular parent interviews started in June 1981 to allow parents to discuss pupils' progress. A gradual move towards greater parental involvement culminated in September 1985 with the first election for parent and teacher governors to join the new joint governing body for the two schools.

The National Curriculum was introduced to all schools in September 1989 and was the start of a revolution in English education. The requirements for assessment and recording of pupils' progress and the reaction to 'bureaucracy and interference' which this produced led to considerable debate and ill-feeling amongst educationalists. Teacher training days also started in September 1989. These were initially called "Baker Days" after the Secretary for Education at that time. The stress of the new demands was further heightened by national testing of children at seven and eleven and the publication of league tables of results.

Stretton school classroom 1961

More changes were to follow: a system of local management of schools, which gave more power to governors to manage their own budget, came into force in April 1992.

The County had already floated an idea in 1990 to reorganise schools, where possible back to all-through primary schools for 4 to 11 year olds. Fears on the outcome of this led to the new governing body at Stretton proposing in December 1992 that Knightlow should 'go it alone' and merge in September 1993. This was originally supported by the County and the Church but subsequently it was decided to wait for the County reorganisation.

In fact the proposals ultimately put forward by the County in May 1994 reopened wounds from the previous reorganisation in the 1970s, often making local discussion difficult. The eventual outcome, to be implemented in September 1996, was to form three all-through primary schools at Wolston, Ryton and Stretton. The main effect would be to remove Ryton junior school age children from the roll at Stretton - only time would tell if all three schools would be financially viable.

In December 1995 Mrs Large retired after sixteen years at the helm and Mr Hillman was asked to run both schools through to reorganisation. He was subsequently invited to take up headship of the new Primary School. Little building work was necessary for reorganisation but an additional classroom to house the reception class is still only on the drawing board, with the result that in 1999 the former first school building is still in use for this purpose.

1970's - 80's

"We had to take three pairs of shoes to the First School: one for outdoors, one for indoors and one for games."

"There was no more corporal punishment."

"We took part in the Road Safety Competition every year - we won once and Mr Hillman bought us all chocolate bars."

"At playtime we had a tuck shop where we could buy crisps and biscuits."

"I remember being terrorised by the coachdrivers who took us swimming. One was like a Russian athlete - she made us all get off the coach once on the London Road."

"We had school pets. There were so many gerbils, we were allowed to keep two. Once we had the school hamster home for the weekend and it escaped into the central heating duct. My sister was hysterical."

"We were more innocent then. When we had lessons about reproduction, some-one asked how long it took. When the teacher answered, 'As long as you like' – a boy said he would take a flask and sandwiches with him."

"It was great when it snowed because the roads were dangerous and we were sent home."

Knightlow School trip to France in 1984.

Mr Hillman, pupils and guests celebrating the 200 year anniversary in 1989.

The former first school building is also used for new ventures which have started since reorganisation: a Before and After School Club and a full-time nursery have been established by the Knightlow Child Care organisation. Although both ventures are fee paying, they are run under the auspices of the School Governors.

The school continues to flourish: residential trips to Southam, Offchurch, Marle Hall in North Wales and Normandy have became very much part of the Knightlow tradition. In April 1998, both staff and pupils weathered the Ofsted inspection system with commendable results, the National Literacy strategy was introduced in September of the same year and in 1999 the National Numeracy Strategy is about to start. As the Millennium approaches, computer systems have been introduced to meet the needs of future generations.

Year 6 at Marle Hall, 1999.

SCHOOLDAY MEMORIES 1990'S

A SELECTION OF SOME OF THE THINGS THE CHILDREN
OF KNIGHTLOW SCHOOL WROTE IN 1999:
If I left school tomorrow, I would remember:

"The interesting topics we learn. Complicated maths. Science.
Writing stories. Really good books."

"Computers and what we have learned to do on them, like touch typing
and spreadsheets."

"How to model clay. Different types of pencils to use for drawing.

Scissors nearly always being missing."

"We play instruments too - we are working on rhythm and sound. Playing the
recorder but you need a lot of puff."

"All the goals I score in football. Cross country running and athletics.
Long jump and the sand in your socks."

"Pond dipping, when Matthew caught 20 fish and 2 snails and I caught a
dead bumble bee and we all nearly fell in."

"Girls at play time and lunch time who beat boys up. I had no part in this."

"Trips like Offchurch, when I fell in the pond, Ironbridge, Coventry Cathedral
and a Hindu temple."

"When we all went to the pantomime. Twycross Zoo."

"Trying to remember words in French. Time penalties."

"My cousin goes to this school and my Auntie teaches year 5."

"My friends who always stood by me and my teachers who were always nice.
Hopefully I will get a job because of them."

"If I left school tomorrow, I would miss it loads."

8

WORKING ON THE LAND
AGRICULTURAL LIFE OF THE VILLAGE

From its very beginning through to the mid-20th century, Stretton was mainly an agricultural community. In this chapter, we look at the way in which the land around the village was first cultivated and note the changes which have brought about the farms and fields which we see today. Finally with a collection of anecdotes and observations, we shall take a glimpse at rural life over the last 80 years.

THE FIRST FIELDS

We have already established that Stretton was originally settled by Anglo-Saxons who had migrated from northern Europe bringing with them a method of farming known as open field agriculture. In its earliest form, the land was cleared to form two large fields which were cultivated jointly by all of the villagers. To maintain the fertility of the land, crops were rotated and each field in turn was left fallow for one year. Animals would be pastured on the fallow field and wasteland, with separate meadows being kept for hay.

It is likely that the Anglo-Saxons who founded Stretton first cleared two open fields around their original settlement near Well Head. These were probably located either side of the Fosse Way.

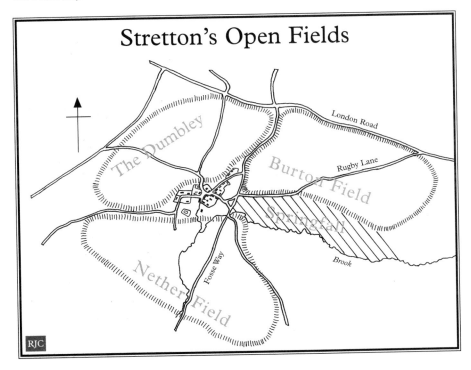

Stretton's Open Fields

In the later Anglo-Saxon period, neighbouring communities were beginning to compete for land to support an increasing population. To produce more food from the land already cleared, the two-field rotation was gradually replaced by a three field system in which land was left fallow only every third year.

In Stretton's case, the original two fields would first have been extended to the west and east until, like other settlements in the midlands, a third field became necessary. This was located on the south side of the village.

HOW THE OPEN FIELDS WERE DIVIDED

The open fields were not ploughed in the modern style through the full length without a break. They were instead divided into sections small enough for ox-teams and ploughed in a direction which would encourage drainage. Consequently, they resembled a patchwork quilt.

The sections were divided into strips of roughly one acre and each villager was allocated a number of these in each of the fields. The strips were ploughed in a way which formed ridges. Where these were subsequently turned over to pasture, the ridges and the furrows between them became 'fossilised' and can still be seen in many areas to this day.

Owing to modern ploughing, most of Stretton's ridges and furrows are no longer visible. However, if you take the footpath beside the Shoulder of Mutton or that from Plott Lane to Freeboard Lane, and look carefully you will still see clear signs of those earlier times patterned in the ground. Fortunately, early aerial photography has recorded the fields which were formerly ridged.

THE LAND UNDER CULTIVATION IN THE 11TH CENTURY

The entry for Stretton in the Domesday Book of 1086 confirms that by the late 11th century the village was already a well-established agricultural community.

From this record, we discover that at that time there were about 600 acres under cultivation. If we imagine this as a circle of land with a diameter of over a mile, we can see that a significant part of the present parish had already been cleared for agriculture.

In addition, the value of the land in 1086 is recorded as having doubled since 1066, indicating that the village had thrived despite the Conquest.

THE OPEN FIELDS THROUGH THE MEDIAEVAL PERIOD

The Normans may have taken political control but do not appear to have radically changed the way the land was farmed. The efficiency of the Anglo-Saxon three-field system prevailed and that form of agriculture did not change significantly for several hundred years. The annual cycle of allocating strips of land to each villager and rotating the use of the three fields continued until the beginning of the 18th century.

The original three open fields in Stretton were known as the Dumbley, Burton Field and the Nether Field. The original meadowlands were probably in an area which was called the Springfall. Their position is shown on the map on page 71.

There would have been a gradual expansion of the large fields as more land was progressively claimed from the waste. But this process was limited by the available land

Map showing the fields around Stretton

Aerial photography has highlighted those which were 'ridged'

RJC

> *"One day the headteacher said, 'There's a swarm of bees in Plott Lane. Go and fetch it.' I climbed up a tree at the bottom of the Dumbley with Jack Blencowe to fetch it but the branch broke and we landed in the ditch with about 50,000 bees. We didn't get stung - we ran so fast they couldn't catch us!"*
>
> *"Mr Lewin had 2 or 3 'Daisy' air guns. We didn't use lead shot but pressed a potato in the end which cut a perfect pellet so we could play Cowboys without anyone getting hurt."* (c1915-20)

between parishes and the need to maintain common land for pasturage. In Stretton, there appears to have been a tract of common heathland by Freeboard Lane and woods towards Princethorpe.

OWNERSHIP OF THE LAND

Under the feudal system introduced by the Normans, the King granted land to his barons who in turn assigned manors to their followers. However, all land ultimately belonged to the crown: villagers did not own their strips of land but were allocated them in return for working on the lord of the manor's domain.

> *"The highlight of one birthday party was seeing the ring put through the pig's nose."* (c1930-40)

As the feudal system gradually disappeared it was superseded by a money-based system of rents and wages. For example, in Stretton as early as 1262, the lord of the manor, Thomas de Garshale, transferred some land and buildings to Robert Heriz for 20 marks in silver and a rent of 1d or a pair of white gloves. Shortly after, Robert relet the same for 30 marks.

The system of land tenure evolved through the 15th to 17th centuries when land in the village is recorded as being sold rather than let but the open field system remained in operation. However, throughout this period, farming self-sufficiency was gradually being

> *"In September, the children of the village would queue up for a bag of pears from the trees in the back garden. The old pear tree still growing against the wall at Church View, No 6 Brookside, was planted around 1865 by Daniel Parrott, a great gardener. Many old fruit trees were around this area at the beginning of the century and it was generally believed to be the old Manor House orchard."*
>
> *"There was a 'sparrow club' in the village after a plague of sparrows and rats. Mr Barnwell gave us a halfpenny for a sparrow's head and a penny for a rat's tail. When they thrashed the corn, I would catch about a dozen rats and take them to Old Frank - a shilling was a lot of money."* (c1915-20)

replaced by emerging markets for agricultural produce. By the end of the 17th century, the change to the economics of agriculture could not be ignored and, the principal land owners in Stretton were considering the enclosure of the village's open fields to create more productive individual farms which could better supply the market.

> *"Cows were frequently brought through the streets for milking and horses for preparation for the day's work in the field."*
>
> *"Milking was done by the light of candles."*
> (c1930-40)

THE ENCLOSURE

From about the 16th century onwards, villages throughout England began to enclose their open fields and redistribute the multiple strips in blocks of land often called 'closes.' Where the principal land holders all wished to enclose the land, this was done by agreement but where there was opposition the proposers would petition Parliament for an Act to authorise the enclosure of their village.

An agreement to enclose Stretton's open fields was signed and sealed in 1704. Through

this agreement, the three large open fields were divided into the smaller fields which remain, largely unaltered, in the pattern of hedgerows around the village today.

In the same way as the great fields had names, the closes were individually titled. A few of these are shown on the map on page 76.

The farms which are an integral part of the modern village were mostly created through the enclosure of the common fields. Within the immediate village, these

> *"Most cottages kept a pig in a sty in the back yard. After slaughter, the carcass would be salted, covered in muslin and hung on beams in the washhouse."*
>
> *"If word went round that a pig was to be killed, the children would race to the appointed spot to watch."* (c1930-40)

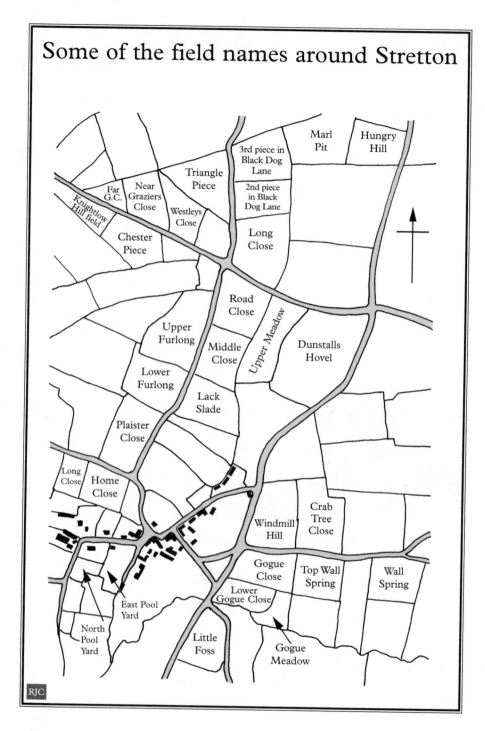

Some of the field names around Stretton

Marl Pit

Hungry Hill

3rd piece in Black Dog Lane

Triangle Piece

2nd piece in Black Dog Lane

Far G.C.

Near Graziers Close

Knightlow Hill field

Westleys Close

Chester Piece

Long Close

Road Close

Upper Furlong

Middle Close

Upper Meadow

Dunstalls Hovel

Lower Furlong

Lack Slade

Plaister Close

Long Close

Home Close

Crab Tree Close

Windmill Hill

Gogue Close

Top Wall Spring

Wall Spring

Lower Gogue Close

East Pool Yard

North Pool Yard

Little Foss

Gogue Meadow

RJC

included Moor Farm, Yew Tree Farm, Church Farm and Manor Farm where land was allocated to their 18th century owners around an existing house. In other cases such as Asylum Farm, the blocks of enclosed land were away from the village. This eventually caused new homes to be built on those plots, creating many of the outlying farms and smallholdings we see today.

JOSEPH ELKINGTON AND HIS SYSTEM OF LAND DRAINAGE

The Elkington family is recorded in Stretton Parish records from around the 17th century and owned land throughout the county. A monument in the churchyard at Stretton bears the name, barely decipherable, of Joseph Elkington "who greatly benefited his country by the introduction of his system of draining land." Around 1764 the Elkington family land in Princethorpe had become exceptionally wet, "causing the rotting of several hundred sheep". Joseph realised that the wetness was often lying further below the surface than it was possible to reach with normal drains and discovered a method of applying an auger to bore further into the earth and drain off deeper water.

Around 1795 the incredible success of the Warwickshire farmer in developing the drainage system had reached the ears of higher authorities with the result that an edict was issued to Parliament that "His Majesty would be graciously pleased to give directions for issuing to Mr Joseph Elkington, as an inducement to discover his mode of draining, not exceeding the sum of £100".

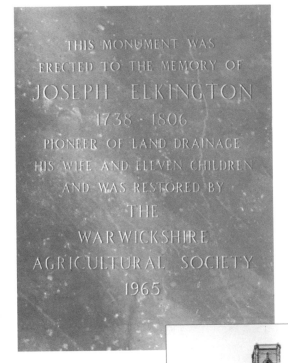

The memorial to Joseph Elkington and his wife and eleven children.

In 1796 Elkington was appointed to work for the Board of Agriculture and in 1797 a description of his land drainage system was published, the first of three editions. He also travelled throughout England and Scotland planning and supervising drainage for farms, quarries and mines. He died in Staffordshire in 1806. The Stretton tomb marks not only his name but the grave of his wife and eleven children.

THE ROSE ESTATE SALE

By the early 1900s, a large part of the agricultural land in Stretton had been acquired by the Rose Estate. In a single momentous auction sale held on 7 July 1919, Church Farm, Yew Tree Farm, Moor Farm and a number of smallholdings totalling 438 acres were sold in lots. They have remained in separate ownership since that time but only Church Farm remains a working farm. The land from the others has been transferred and they are now private homes.

MEMORIES OF LIFE IN THE RURAL COMMUNITY

Observations of a country village such as Stretton are enriched by childhood memories and to some extent recollections of a lifestyle which no longer exists. But Stretton is a living community and even today's younger generation have memories which are dear to them. The history of rural life in the 20th century is in the form of quotations from all age groups.

"Mr Burden was one of several pig-killers and he had 15 children. He snared 4 or 5 rabbits everyday and another mainstay was pigeon pie. Potatoes were cooked in a copper and each child took a share. A walk to market for spoiled vegetables and apples ensured that all the children were well fed."
(c1930-40)

"Tom Grant would collect geese, duck and hens' eggs in his bowler hat which would then be returned to his head until he got home."

"Old Frank would give me a shilling for a dozen golden carp which we used to catch in a pond up Plott Lane. He used them for bait for catching pike in Frankton Pools." (c1915-20)

HARD WORK IN THE FIELDS c 1930-40

"They did the threshing in a field by the Hillies and kept all the straw in a barn nearby."

"Irish workers came to pick swedes, mangels and sugar beet, but we village mothers and children picked potatoes to earn money for our winter boots and shoes."

"We worked very long hours and I was only paid 12s 6d for 7 days. I worked 24 years, non-stop, without a holiday."

"People had to be strong to survive. My Grandad could dig potatoes out faster than I could pick them up."

"When Harry Howkins' wife developed a poisoned thumb, he took the bone out with his pocket knife which left her thumb about twice the width it should have been. With 13 children to look after, she was still faster than anyone at skinning a rabbit."

"We were always off rabbiting, mushrooming or nutting. We always brought something home for the pot. We knew where the wild strawberries were in Frankton Wood and could find the white orchids - the purple ones were too easy."
(c1915-20)

Photograph of Jesse Boneham and a team of horses at Moor Farm, Stretton on Dunsmore c1917.

"When my grandfather killed a pig for people, I would go round with him. My job was to get the toenails off."

"I can remember an occasion when it was time for one of our pigs to be killed and my mother came in crying her eyes out and the pig was carted off to the garage along with a big tin bath. I never really understood what the bath was for."

"When the pig had to be slaughtered there was a great black sad feeling of doom over the house but, within an hour or two, I would be happily playing football with the unfortunate pig's bladder."
(c1930-40)

CATTLE DISEASES C 1930-40

"There was one outbreak of anthrax in the 1930s - a bullock owned by a local farmer. The dead animal was placed in a cart and taken to a site on the Fosse. Some men and P C Anderton stayed with the animal all night. The next morning they dug a huge hole, put some coal in, set light to it and tipped the bullock into the fire to burn it."

"In this instance only one animal was infected but in an anthrax outbreak around the 1950s there was an anthrax pit to the rear of Frog Hall for disposal of carcasses."

"'Foot and Mouth' disease also affected animals in the village resulting in the destruction of entire herds. A ministry valuer would assess the worth of the animals and compensation was paid. Although the amount received was fair, farmers suffered because there would be no calves for the following year."

"If 'Foot and Mouth' was found, the entire herd and all other cattle in a three-mile radius would be destroyed. Once Rugby market was closed for 8 or 10 weeks to stop movement of animals."

FARMERS TALES C 1930-40

One local bull was very gentle and popular with the children; they would ride him when the farmer collected the cows for milking.

When me and old Clegg Howard worked for Joe Howkins, we sat in the old barn for dinner. Clegg would sit down and undo his lunch wrapped in a white linen napkin. He would shout "Bobby" and a little robin would fly in, settle on the toe of Clegg's boot and he would feed it. It didn't matter how long the interval between us going down there, it could be weeks, that little robin always appeared.

The animals generally had a much nicer life than they would do nowadays. They were fed on a variety of scraps from the house. Today they would be classed as organic.

I used to help make butter every Thursday and I can remember collecting water in two buckets on a yoke. There was no shortage of water because everyone had a pump and there was a spring at Well Head.

"After the war many people were able to travel to work at Rootes in Ryton (now Peugeot) and at the Baginton Airport site where wages were higher, leaving fewer people to work on the land."

"The worst thing nowadays about living in a village is the smell when they spread the slurry on the fields."

"In the 1980s children would spend hours in 'Paradise', an area of scrub between Orchard Way and the Plott Lane playing field, possibly part of the old Manor House orchard. It was full of bushes, flowers and an assortment of wild life, including a muntjac deer. Sadly it has now been cleared."

"We children from Manor Drive played in the meadows behind the Shoulder of Mutton. There were trees to climb and the brook was lovely then along Coffin Walk. We often took a bottle of squash and sandwiches and would catch minnows."

"Mum always took us to pick blackberries in Plott Lane at the end of the summer holidays before the farmer cut the hedgerow. We had separate plastic bags to fill and we each made a pie when we got home."

John Burden, hedge-laying near Princethorpe.

"Mrs George would always bring bunches of fresh cut holly to the Christmas bazaar. We used to make wreaths with holly and ivy tied around wire coat hangers. Now they are ready-made wreaths."

"In the 1950s Gilbert Harris kept a goat farm of 100 animals which produced 10,000 gallons of milk a year, employing six girls to tend the herd."

"Help at harvest time was frequently hired from other areas after the war, one man coming each summer from Bilton and staying until autumn."

THE 1990s

Farming is no longer the main source of income for the village but despite a changing world, we still see evidence of our agricultural roots. Organisations continue to promote crafts and we observe country celebrations (see Chapter 13, Customs and Folklore). A greater awareness of the environment has aroused a spirit of 'make do and mend', notably the collection of waste paper, aluminium and glass at the Fosse playing field for recycling.

Although there are now vacant allotments which no-one has time to tend, those which are occupied are lovingly maintained in the traditional way. There has also been an increasing interest in gardening. In 1995 this led to the first Stretton Open Gardens event when eleven gardens were open to the public. 200 visitors took part and the afternoon raised £400 towards the tennis court project. It has now become an annual event.

THE 1990s

"We may not be allowed to pick primroses and bluebells any more but we still pick sloes for sloe gin!"

"Every year my mother makes wine from elderflowers. When I took it to University, they thought it was 'trendy.'"

"One of the nice things about living in a village is that people share produce with each other. Even today you can find a bag of damsons, a few tomatoes, plants or a stack of firewood left on your doorstep. And if you are ill, you're likely to find a cake or a box of Peggy Richardson's home-made shortbread!"

Photograph of Jane and twins Paul and Ian Simpson feeding lambs at Moor Farm, Stretton on Dunsmore in 1966.

9

TRADING FOR A LIVING
COMMERCIAL LIFE IN THE VILLAGE

In a rural community such as Stretton, agriculture was the predominant source of work until the industrial revolution brought new ways of earning a living in nearby towns. The village would have been largely self-supporting until the late 18th century and served not only by agricultural workers but by craftsmen and women, such as builders, carpenters, milliners and dressmakers, shopkeepers, wheelwrights and blacksmiths, and those we now classify as professionals, for instance the vicar, teacher and surgeon. Records for the village show that others worked in the mining and processing of natural materials and some were domestic servants to the more wealthy landowners. With no welfare state until the 20th century, women were mainly occupied with the household and were obliged to provide direct care of children, the sick and the elderly; they frequently supplemented their income with other work from home such as dressmaking and laundry. With a growing population in the 18th century, Stretton operated in fact as a small town and its history lists examples of most commercial activities.

1763

Early examples of these activities are shown on the map of the Duke of Buccleuch's estate which mentions a shoemaker (John Burton), two blacksmiths (Thomas Judd & William Brown), a brickyard, gravel pit and 'painthouse'. Up to the late 18th century, those who produced goods were also the retailers and shops would not have been run as we know them today. Numerous other essential services would have been provided by individuals on a hire basis.

1841

The 1841 census shows how the village was developing into a thriving community: in addition to numerous farmers, we see a wide variety of craftsmen, including three wheelwrights, three blacksmiths, several carpenters,

Borsley's store operated for over a century, first under Mr T Borsley, then by two of his four sons (Harold and Bert).

two bricklayers, a plumber, a cooper (barrel maker), three shoemakers, four tailors and two dressmakers. A cattle dealer, excise officer and a surgeon are also listed. No bakery is mentioned, suggesting that baking was still done at home.

Shops were in existence in the village but were frequently little more than front rooms with items for sale spread out on a table. However, this census records two butchers, a grocer and a draper who by then would have had shops of some kind.

Three years prior to the census, Stretton acquired its first Post Office when a Mr Powell applied for the penny post to be brought to the village. The postal authorities initially considered that the expenses would exceed the income but agreed to introduce the post to the village for one year if Mr Powell would reimburse them for any loss. On 28th November 1838 a receiving house was set up at the Black Dog. The location was considered "a convenient point" for the district, a decision indignantly disputed by the village of Wolston who did not receive its own postal service until 1839.

When this photograph was taken, the Post Office was in the house on the right.

1850

Trade directories in the 19th and 20th centuries listed those tradesmen who paid to be included. Whilst it did not list every commercial activity, White's Directory of Warwickshire for 1850 indicates that the village was becoming more prosperous and now boasted an ironmonger, glazier, veterinary surgeon, timber merchant and several carriers (carters). The Post Office still thrived under Mr John Hudson Bagshaw.

1900

By 1900 the variety of trades became even wider and Kelly's Directory for that year added a surveyor, hurdlemaker, market gardener, two bakers and a horse clipper to the list. While most services may already have been available in the village, the start of the 20th century saw a greater specialisation to meet the demands of the increasing population and contemporary life.

The old 'Electric Bakery' in Brookside.

Two names now become prominent in commercial life: Wilcox and Borsley.

THE WILCOX FAMILY

There is evidence of the Wilcox family living in the village since the 17th century as farmers and in the early 19th century as butchers but in 1893 we see the first mention of the Wilcox bakery. In the early part of the 20th century the bakehouse, which is now part of Brookside Stores, used an oven heated by coke for both bread and cakes. As was common practice at that time, local ladies could also pay to cook food in the oven which they had prepared themselves. The bakery was later converted to electricity.

In 1911 the Wilcox family built a large house at the Knob, said to be a 21st birthday present for their son, Frank. This became the venue for many village events, including garden parties and concerts. On the death of Mr Wilcox, Mrs Wilcox moved to "The Castle", a small folly in Cut-Throat Lane designed by her daughter, Marjorie. Frank Wilcox, an extrovert of legendary character, bought Yew Tree Hall.

> Mr Wilcox had 4 carts delivering bread to all the surrounding villages.
> Next to Borsleys' storeroom was an open yard, with two sheds where the baker put the vehicles.
> When they came back from delivering bread and cakes to the various villages, if it was dark, they didn't unload them until morning;
>
> *"Us hungry lads could smell them cakes a hundred yards away.*
> *Mrs Wilcox caught some of the lads raiding one night and shouted,*
> *'Come out of there; I know who you are!*
> *Who are you?' "*

Mrs Wilcox became well-known as a benefactor. On the first of November, All Saints Day, she was in the habit of making a birthday cake which she would fill with sweets for the children "on the Church's birthday'. In 1939 she started a fund for a village fire pump.

In 1953 she presented a handsome banner to the Mothers Union, in silver brocade bearing an embroidered picture of the Virgin and Child. In 1954 came the gift of a beautiful frontal for the church communion table. She died around 1960 at almost 100 years of age and is buried in Stretton with her husband and son.

BORSLEY'S STORE

Borsley's store operated for over a century, first under Mr T Borsley, brother of Emily Wilcox, then by two of his four sons (Harold and Bert). The shop, which was located on the Green and is now occupied by the Hallmark graphics business, was eventually sold outside the family and closed in the 1980s. In the early part of the 20th century, the establishment was considered high-class, with customers from a wide area placing regular orders which would be boxed and delivered. Goods to established customers were paid for on account. As in grocery shops everywhere at that time, all transactions for those who visited the shop were dealt with over a counter. Sugar, rice, oats, and many other items were sold 'loose' and had to be weighed and wrapped separately. Bacon and ham were cut from the shoulder or leg to requirement, cheese and butter cut from a block. Salt was also sold in blocks while soap and candles were supplied without packaging, wrapped simply in newspaper. Spices, loose tea and dried fruits were kept in drawers to be scooped out to order. Biscuits were on display in large, glass-fronted tins and weighed in bags, with broken biscuits sold at a reduced price. Treacle, sherry and vinegar came in barrels with a tap, the customer frequently providing their own container. It was to be many years before packaged 'provisions' were to be seen in such stores or customers allowed to serve themselves.

"The Wilcox men delivered bread and cakes in a horse and trap all round the neighbouring villages - a delivery round to isolated farms would take all day but we always had a hot cottage loaf and cheese followed by macaroons or fairy cakes. I delivered groceries for Borsleys in a Ford van but that wasn't so good as we had no free lunch!"

Borsley's store as many people will remember it.

1920-1940

The years after the First World War brought unemployment for many. With its rural economy, Stretton was fortunate but saw evidence of the plight of others. In the 1930s locals remember hunger marchers passing by from the North on their way to Parliament and a continuous stream of tramps travelling along the London Road, moving from one workhouse to another.

Commercial life in the village, however, continued unabated. Over the next 20 years we find more local names in businesses still remembered today. Bourton Page, Dolman, Paget, Shelswell, Quarterman, Scattergood, Simcox and Wise are among those listed in the directory and remain in childhood memories.

By now the variety of services had grown tremendously.

View from the Village Centre towards School Lane at the end of the last century.

D. Wise's sweet shop in Brookside with a sign that states 'Licensed to sell tobacco.'

In Church Hill, the Misses Scattergood and Thompson ran a haberdashery shop. A small cycle business, Nelson & Floradine, also operated here and at another cottage were George and Harry Paget, who were carpenters and undertakers. At various times, the Village Green supported Jessett's fish and chip shop, the Simcox shoe shop and Shelswell's sweet shop. The cottages beyond the Oak and Black Dog were home to several establishments: Mr Gilbert ran a shoe repair business in Brookside and later in Knob Hill. At the bottom of the hill Mrs Grant not only made delicious icecream, ginger beer and lemonade but was famous for potions. Her boil cure was in great demand, with a recipe so secret that no-one was allowed into the kitchen when she prepared it.

A sweet shop in the same row and favourite of many children was run by 'Granny' Wise, whose husband was one of

> *"Mrs Quinney the chimney sweep was known as a very tough lady, travelling around the villages with a bike and trailer. She was a popular figure at society weddings, presenting horseshoes in her sweep's outfit - an old tradition thought to bring luck. When she married Bert Quinney, they kept the reception going for a week, with tables laid under a tarpaulin. There was never another reception like that in Stretton."*

two coal merchants. Mr Quarterman at the top of Knightlow Hill, was the other and also used his lorry to provide a very different service: the lower section of the lorry would be ingeniously combined with the roof section of a charabanc to form a bus for outings to the seaside.

A butcher's shop (Bourton Page) was located at the bottom of School Lane and a market garden lay opposite Dunsmore House, with a barn and greenhouses on the site of the present-day bungalows. The secret of Bill Watson's fine fruit and vegetables was said to be the contents of the village 'night soil' buckets which were emptied on Friday nights. Produce was taken to market by cart - but only if he could catch his spirited horse on market day.

Other services included saw mills in Frankton Lane, another fish and chip shop opposite Dunsmore House, Mr Edwards the barber, Parrotts the builders, Mrs Quinney the lady chimney sweep and Mr Coleman who supplied icecream from his motorbike and sidecar.

With better transport and roads, many more commercial travellers now visited the village to sell their wares on a regular basis, providing items such as paraffin and oil, hardware, drapery, creams and potions, greengrocery and wet fish.

Although most items could be purchased without leaving the village, on occasions it was necessary to go further afield. The carrier, with stables behind 'The Haven' at the bottom of Church Hill, provided a lift to Coventry, Rugby, Warwick or Banbury but an excursion would take up most of the day.

John Anderton, the village butcher, in his shop doorway.

> *"Mrs Turrell gave piano lessons in her cottage at the bottom of Knob Hill in the 1920s at 1s 6d a lesson."*

1945-1990

The original Post Office on the London Road had long since moved to the centre of the village and a variety of locations before it found its current home and developed into a general store. At the turn of the century it was located in cottages near to the Oak and Black Dog and around 1913 it was in Church Hill. It then moved to the Village Green where it was located in the same row as it is today, but at the opposite end. For many years it also provided an office for the Midland Red Parcel Service. Villagers will remember proprietors' names such as Turrell, Paget, Thompson, Law, Lovell, Stergen, Hunter, Combes and Foster.

Immediately after the war Stretton continued to maintain a number of shops but significant changes occurred. One of these was the supply of dairy produce. Before the war,

milk had been supplied direct from the farms but new requirements for pasteurization to reduce tuberculosis meant that most farms were not sufficiently equipped to continue direct sales. Stretton was fortunate in finding a modern alternative when in the early 1950s Heinz Kittendorf installed the necessary equipment for a dairy at Well Head. Now closed, the business once

The Stretton Dairy in Brookside

"The saw mill started in the 1920s in Frankton Lane removed most of the trees in Frankton Wood. I can still see the horse dragging the timber along the clearings. The trees used to be so thick they met over the road - it was like walking in a tunnel."

"Around 1922 I collected and delivered the papers, meeting the Midland Red bus outside the Dun Cow at teatime and then taking the Birmingham Gazette around the village."

"By the time I got to old Jacob Garrett's cottage at Well Head, it would be 8pm and he would moan because he was last to read the news."

"Mary Manton, a little old lady, was noted for her pork pies which would keep for weeks without a fridge. They can't make 'em like that nowadays."

employed twelve full-time and part-time workers and maintained a number of delivery vans covering some twenty villages.

Such delivery vehicles and the tremendous post-war demand for cars meant a need for petrol pumps. A hand operated pump was originally located outside Borsleys and before long the village had gained the Edgeway service station and two service stations to the east of the Monument. Public and private transport now began to improve dramatically and reaching the developing towns of Coventry, Leamington and Rugby was no longer time-consuming. Many villagers also worked in the towns.

Seal's Gift Shop in School Lane in the 1970s.

> "Our mothers gave us dire warnings not to spend our church collection if the ice cream man came before Sunday service."

> "Percy Holmes delivered ice cream on a bike, cycling all the way from Coventry, where he had collected it."

> "Tom Grant's wife used to make lovely ice cream; she wore a wig which fascinated us because it always slipped when she bent to get the ice cream out of the tub."

The Wilcox bakery had closed and bread was delivered to the Post Office Stores and Borsleys by larger bakery companies. Fresh meat was still available until the 1980s from John Anderton, who had been apprenticed to Mr Bourton Page and ultimately ran the shop at the bottom of Church Hill originally owned by Mr Dolman.

> "Health and safety were not great issues of the day before the war. Mrs Shelswell would keep the aspirins safe by sitting on them. A quarter of sweets would be deftly dispensed with the same hands that a few moments previously had been making up the fire."

Evidence of a more affluent society came in the form of two hairdressing salons (one of which still operates as 'Country Styles') and Seal's gift shop. The latter had been converted from the old butcher's shop at the bottom of School Lane and sold fancy goods and hardware.

> "My Dad loved his baccy - black twist. He would say, 'Go down to Mrs Wise's and fetch me an ounce and tell her I'll pay on Friday.' He smoked an ounce a day all his life."

> "Mrs Thompson at the Post Office had the only telephone in the village. If she was in a good mood, she would let you phone for the doctor. If not, it was a case of a quick dash to Wolston on your bike."

Delivery men remained part of village life into the 1990s with the familiar sight of vegetable vans driven by Jesse Quinney and John Simmonds. Changing habits in shopping, however, the closure of Borsleys grocers shop in the 1980s and John Anderton's retirement as village butcher have left only Brookside Stores and the Hallmark graphics

The village in the 1960s.

business. The empty butcher's shop can still seen alongside 'The Haven' but the bustling commercial activity around the village green is no more.

At the end of the 1990s, a number of businesses still operate from houses, including painters and decorators, song writing, builders, catering, mobile hairdressers, dressmakers, a repair garage and gardening services. With the advent of computers, an increasing number of people also work from offices at home.

"On Saturdays Mr Such would come with his greengrocer's cart, with a light at the front and back. If you were lucky your mum would give you tuppence and you could buy bananas."

"At one time not only 2 fish and chip shops but also a van supplied fast food in Stretton around the 1940s."

"When Mrs Lewin opened a fish and chip shop in School Lane, my brother and I would peel potatoes. Our pay was the first packet of chips."

INDUSTRY IN THE SOIL

Stretton's natural resources include large deposits of sand and gravel. The Brook, a small tributary of the River Avon, effectively divides the village into two types of soil. On the east side, where the soil is sandy and full of gravel, these resources have been well used for many years and have provided a good source of income for the village.

As early as 1763, the Duke of Buccleuch's records list a gravel pit at the top of Knob Hill. In the following century, the Parrott family quarried both sand and gravel until 1880 when the pit ran out. The materials were used for work at Boughton Hall, Princethorpe Priory and part of the Wood House Hotel at Princethorpe. On the south side of Rugby Lane, the ground falls away steeply where extensive workings took place in the 19th century. Two pits were worked on the Fosse until around 1900. In the early part of the century Knob Hill was bought from Mrs Howkins by the Council. So good were the deposits that villagers were allowed to exchange a barrow of good earth for a barrow of sand or gravel. The site of one of the pits can still be seen in the garden of The Knob, the large house built by the Wilcox family in 1911 and a further sand pit was located between Primrose Hill and Knob Hill.

> "Three milkmen delivered milk in the early part of the century one using a pony and trap, another a bicycle. Milk was ladled out of buckets, often with hay seeds or pieces of straw floating on the top."

> "The front door of Wise's sweet shop was also the door to the living room. Often the family would be having a meal when a customer called but someone would always get up to serve a halfpenny-worth of sweets."

GYPSUM

Around the junction of School Lane and Plott Lane, large deposits of gypsum clay were extensively mined until the early 1900s. Gypsum is an hydrated form of calcium sulphate which occurs naturally from deposits of fossilised sea creatures once found beneath the bank which now forms the Dunsmore heath. This is burned, mixed with water and used for plaster of paris and for the building industry. The remains of the mining were still evident until recent times as mounds on the bend of School Lane, in the area once known as 'The Hillies'.

> "Villagers were also employed in mining outside the village. A number of young men worked at Binley coal pit."

> "I remember fetching cement and lime in hessian bags from Stockton works. The lime was freshly ground and really hot."

Two brick kilns, said to be six feet tall, were used to burn the clay. The mine was eventually closed when a sudden flood filled the workings, causing the miners to leave their tools and run for their lives. They were lucky to escape at all since it is said that the mine was once run by a formidable lady who would not allow her husband and sons to come up from the shafts until they had done a good day's work. A 'plaster pit' is shown on the 1763 map, together with cottages at The Hillies which were said to be occupied by the workers.

Such was the size of the deposits, which varied in colour from a pastel blue to a deep green, that large numbers of shafts were sunk in an area extending as far as what is now Hill Crescent.

Warrens of tunnels are thought to still exist under the village. It is said that a horse and cart, a carriage and four and even a van have all fallen into holes and that the carriage was never recovered. To this day, holes still appear in footpaths and roads, the most recent being after flooding in 1998.

The natural resources of the village encouraged further industry. Lime stone was extensively quarried in 1813 in Stretton and lime kilns are shown in Frankton Woods on a map dated 1886. There was also a tile and brick industry in the village. On the 1763 map, a brickyard is shown to the left of the White Lion Inn (see Chapter 12) on the London road. A brick works, already disused, was located in Frankton Lane on a map dated 1886.

In the 1980s a Rugby sand and gravel company, Steetley Construction, applied for permission to excavate a 39 acre site at the rear of Frog Hall. Appeals were lodged and after many months of legal dispute, permission was ultimately granted. In 1999 excavation work had been carried out over a large area and parts of the site are already being filled in and restored for agricultural use.

Borsleys' store decorated for the coronation of King George VI in 1937.

28th October 1995.

10

BATTLING THROUGH
TIMES OF WAR

S nugly placed in the heart of England, Stretton was relatively untouched by foreign wars until the 20th century. However, the movement of troops would have disrupted this strategic location at intervals.

THE ROMAN INVASION

The main invasion of Britain by the Roman armies began in 43 AD. Within four years they had subdued most of the tribes of Britain as far north as Lincoln and constructed the Fosse Way as a communications link between the northern limit and Exeter.

Although there is no concrete evidence to suggest there was any habitation in the Stretton area at that time, there would certainly have been considerable military movement along the route and between the camps at Chesterton and High Cross as the Romans extended their territory. The occupation lasted for more than 400 years.

THE MEDIAEVAL PERIOD

During Anglo-Saxon times Stretton would certainly have been affected by skirmishes on the borders of English and Danish Mercia and the Dunsmore remained a dangerous area for many centuries. The payment of Wroth Silver to the lords of the Knightlow Hundred for the protection of the villages was first recorded in 1210 (see Chapter 13).

Soldiers would have tramped through Warwickshire along the Fosse Way and the road from Oxford on many occasions through the centuries. In 1485, at the end of the war of the Roses, the decisive Battle of Bosworth was fought less than 20 miles away.

THE 17TH CENTURY

During the seventeenth century Stretton again found itself caught up in the agony of divided loyalties and the dangers of a location in the middle of a civil war, this time between Parliamentarians and Royalists. Men were mustered in Coventry and Warwick. Some local people followed Lord Brooke of Warwick in supporting Oliver Cromwell and Stretton, together with other villages, contributed regular sums to raise cavalry for him. Other local people, mostly the gentry and the Catholics, followed the Earl of Northamptonshire at Compton Wynyates in supporting King Charles I. Throughout the first few years of the war, armies marching to and fro disrupted the rural economy as villagers were forced to provide food, lodging and horses. The first major event in the county was the siege of Warwick castle in August 1642; after the siege was lifted, the Royalists reassembled on Dunsmore Heath and plundered the vicinity. Five days later there was fighting between Southam and Long Itchington which left bodies in the cornfields and bullets embedded in the church at Marton. Afterwards Royalists fled north towards the Dunsmore and Stretton served as a refuge for casualties.

On September 20th 1642 the Earl of Essex, supreme commander, rallied the parliamentary forces on Dunsmore Heath and some of them were quartered at Stretton. It is said that Prince Rupert disguised himself as a pedlar and sold apples to Essex's men on Dunsmore Heath in order to discover information about them. The nearby battles of Edgehill (October 1642) and Naseby (the following year) were also far too close for comfort along the Oxford and London roads and the Fosse. It was ten years before the countryside returned to normal.

> *"Once around 1912 we found a pile of strange bullets in a ditch by Frog Hall. They didn't fit any of our guns. Perhaps they came from earlier times."*

THE 18TH AND 19TH CENTURIES

Although there was no civil war during this period, numerous economic reforms brought riots and unrest throughout Britain in support of civil rights and universal suffrage. In the 19th century, war in Europe and in the British Empire farther afield would have also have taken men from the land, whether by conscription or as volunteers. George Watts, for example, wanted for murder outside Frog Hall, enlisted in the 6th Regiment of Foot, embarking for Bombay on June 5th 1839 (see Chapter 4).

At least two men fought in the Boer War: Harry Manton and William Cleaver. Sadly William died from wounds he received at Reitfontein in 1898 and was buried at Ladysmith.

THE FIRST WORLD WAR 1914-1918

The Parish magazine for October 1914 reads:

"The War is still with us, and likely to be a long struggle, drawing out all the national persistence and pluck. The Parish has 51 men now serving with the Army and Navy, a few of them at the front. W. Simpson, of the 4th Dragoon Guards, is now invalided home, having been twice wounded in France. We shall publish a permanent Roll of Honour of the men who have come forward later on.

A strong War Relief Committee has been appointed, representing every section of the parish and will watch the situation. Cases of real distress (owing to the war) may be brought to the attention of any of the members. A house to house collection will be taken to support this. It is our chance to do a little bit for the country and small offerings are as acceptable as big."

Like every community in Britain, the village was touched by the cruelty of war. Sixteen men from Stretton and Princethorpe were lost in the fighting and their names are listed in the church.

> ### THE KING REVIEWS THE TROOPS 1915
>
> *"I remember the King mounted on a horse standing on the 'Godcake', a triangular piece of turf at the crossroads. One of the other horses bolted, dragging a soldier along the road. I ran up and down the field with my little Union Jack."*

Reviewing the troops on the London Road, 12th March 1915.

A ROYAL VISIT

In 1915 King George V stood to review the troops on the London Road before they left for Gallipoli. All the villagers turned out to watch. It was summer and such a hot day that many soldiers collapsed. There was one local man, Frank Wilcox, in the 29th Division. The memorial to mark the event was unveiled in 1921.

The lime trees were planted along the London Road to commemorate King George V reviewing the 29th Division. These replaced an avenue of elms, which had been planted many years earlier but had been badly damaged in a severe gale in 1912 (see Chapter 11).

MEMORIES FROM THE FIRST WORLD WAR

*"Life for many families in those times was hard and we were near to starving.
The men were all in the army and five of us lived on ten shillings a week.
I remember going to the Manor House most days for a jug of soup.
Mother could hardly drag herself along but would pull swedes for old Billy Grey
for a copper or two. Towards the end of the war she had a job making
munitions at Bluemels in Wolston."*

*"I remember creeping under the table if we thought
German Zeppelins were overhead."*

*"All the men left in the village were old. When Dad was demobbed, we spent as
much time as possible with him but he had been wounded in the leg
and it took a long time to adjust."*

FURTHER MEMORIES FROM THE FIRST WORLD WAR

"Albert Gilbert played the cornet. During the 1914 war, he would come out at night, sit on the white railings by the brook and play all the popular tunes. 'Tipperary', 'Little Grey Home in the West', 'Take Me Back to Dear Old Blighty', 'A Long Long Trail a Winding', etc. Us kids loved it! The outbreak of the Second World War broke up the band."

"I remember Dad coming home on leave in 1916 singing at the top of his voice. My brother and I ran up the road in our nightshirts to meet him."

"The whole family walked to Brandon station to see my father off to Flanders with many tears and much sadness. I was only a child and when he was about 80 years old he told me I'd said "Goodbye, we shan't see you again.""

Guns guarding the monument during the 1920s.

THE SECOND WORLD WAR 1939-1945

The Parish Magazine for January 1940 listed 15 men from Stretton and Princethorpe 'serving King and Country.' The report, written in the very early days of the war, ended with the poignant note: 'Although the war has seemed uneventful to us quiet home-dwellers so far, it is by no means over or won yet and no-one knows what we may still have to go through.'

In fact 54 men and women from Stretton eventually served in the forces in World War II and two servicemen from Stretton and Princethorpe lost their lives.

A War Relief Committee was formed during those years to raise funds for cases of distress. A total of £1,182 was also collected between December 1940 and 1945 which provided each man or woman in the services with a gift of £1 a quarter and allowed an annual party to be organised for their children.

WARTIME LIFE

Shortages affected everyone but conditions in the country were much easier than in the town. Villagers became more self sufficient, keeping pigs and growing more fruit and vegetables.

In 1940, the Ministry of Food announced plans for rationing. Restrictions were initially for bacon, butter and sugar but these were followed by meat, tea and clothing. For some items there were long queues with ration books and for everyone it was a time of make do and mend. In a small community, private arrangements to distribute surplus produce by exchange and barter were common for many goods.

One example was a general shortage of crisps which was overcome locally because the crisps delivery man was always short of eggs. The hens at the 'Shoulder' kept the deliveryman well supplied with eggs and the pub well supplied with crisps.

> ### SERIOUS SHORTAGES
>
> *"If the pub was closed due to lack of beer, and you were 'well in' with the landlord, you would knock on the back door, two or three knocks, and it was opened."*
>
> *"I remember an incident in the Oak & Black Dog when they ran out of beer. Several of us got on our bikes and rode like the devil to the 'Rose & Crown' at Wolston. The landlady served me a pint because she knew me as a butcher - but there was none for the others!"*
>
> *"We would tear from one village to another once we heard a rumour of a pub being open. The amount served was at the landlord's discretion. If strangers went into a pub the landlord would not necessarily serve them, instead serving only his 'regulars'."*

Beer was about 4d a pint at this time but not always available. When beer was on sale at the public houses, men from the village would queue up with jugs and jam jars in order to get a pint. One villager can remember a long queue snaking through the village from the door of the Shoulder of Mutton.

> *"Rationing had less effect on rural areas - we all had access to garden produce. Some families kept ferrets to catch rabbits for extra meat."*

GENERAL CONDITIONS

The bombing of Coventry and the frequent drone of aircraft overhead soon destroyed the peace of the village. 29 bombs dropped around Stretton but none hit houses and, apart from a number of chickens, there were no casualties. Many of the bombs were simply offloaded by German planes passing overhead at the end of their mission. Some of the craters can still be seen in the fields.

THE HOME GUARD

The community was well-guarded by the numerous volunteer services which were in operation. These included the Local Defence Volunteers (LDV), the Air Raid Precautions Service (ARP), Police War Reserve, Home Guard

> *"It was laughable really, the Home Guard would ride around the village with 12 bore shot guns strapped on their backs."*

("Dad's Army") and the Auxiliary Fire Service. Anti-aircraft guns were also in place on the Oxford Road and the London Road. Throughout the country, black-out regulations were in force to make navigation more difficult for enemy aircraft; the village was in total darkness at night and this was closely checked by the A.R.P wardens, which included Harold Borsley and Percy Edmans senior.

The assembly point for Stretton's Local Defence Volunteers was John Mitchell's barn. Three volunteers would keep watch all night. They had a stirrup pump and a bucket of water and were ready for invasion at any time.

> *"The LDV was also known as Look, Duck and Vanish."*

> *"A number of families in the village received evacuees from London and many people from Coventry came to stay overnight in the safety of Stretton during the bombing raids on the city."*

> *"We would sometimes house evacuees from Coventry. We would sleep 16 in our house and there were already 8 of us."*

> *"All our relatives came to stay. In the morning the kitchen would be full of sandwiches for people going back to the city to work."*

> *"As a tiny child, Dame Judy Dench lived on the London Road for several years during the war."*

EVACUEES

In November 1939 the government announced plans for an evacuation programme from cities and built-up areas to the country. Priority was given to children, expectant mothers and the physically disabled. About half of the children of school age in the London area were evacuated, together with around a quarter of the children in the Coventry and Birmingham area of the Midlands.

THE CAMP

In 1941 a chicken farm belonging to Mr Stone was requisitioned for "military purposes" for the princely sum of £12 a year for loss of income. A camp of Nissen huts was duly built in the field where Hill Crescent and Knightlow School are now located. This was originally intended for the Warwickshire regiment but when the British soldiers went abroad, the camp was occupied by the Royal Pioneer Corp and American soldiers.

In 1942 America dispersed troops to stations throughout the country, with many more arriving as the war progressed.

When the last of the Americans left, the huts were empty for a while and at first some were occupied by squatters. Rugby Council took responsibility for the huts and let the rest out for families who had lost their homes during the war. There were 25-30 huts and all were occupied. With poor heating and only one toilet block at the top end of the camp, conditions were not comfortable but so many houses had been destroyed, the occupants had little choice.

These were supposed to be temporary arrangements, for approximately six months, until better housing became available. The families actually remained in the camp for seven years, only moving out in August 1954.

There were also a number of hen houses at Fosse Farm which served as makeshift homes for families 'bombed-out' from Coventry. Today the fireplaces can still be seen in some of the pens.

A VISITING ARMY

"The American officers were all white and the ranks were mostly black. They stayed until they were sent to France, then another lot would arrive. The Americans were mostly friendly and well liked by the villagers, particularly the women. It was always possible to get nylons and cigarettes. In general, the Americans were not quite so popular with the men because they had so much money and were late in entering the war."

"Nissen huts were made of corrugated sheeting with no lining to them so, of course, they were very cold. They had a stove which was used for heating and cooking. Nappies had to be boiled in a bucket on the stove to keep them white. My friend says she was very proud of her nappies."

"One day, an ambulance got bogged down between the rows of Nissen huts when collecting a patient and had to be pulled out by Bill Howe with his tractor."

"When the GIs were confined to camp, I remember watching a line of ladies throwing notes over the hedge... they must have been from Coventry."

"My mother used to do the laundry for the NAAFI at the camp. It was my job to collect the laundry on a Monday morning and take it back on a Tuesday evening."

11

THE HIGHWAYS AND BYWAYS
HISTORY OF THE LANES AND ROADS

The history and social structure of any community is greatly affected by the roads which run through it or are nearby. While lack of transport isolated early villages and forced them to be largely self-sufficient, most communities still depended on a wider area to supply additional goods and labour and provide a market for their own produce. The movement of people through the centuries, as individuals or as armies, and the growth of industry in the Midlands would certainly have had a direct effect on Stretton.

THE FOSSE WAY

The Fosse Way, which runs through our modern village, is not just the oldest road in Stretton but one of the oldest in the country. The Roman occupation of Britain started in 43 AD with the construction of the Fosse Way beginning around 47 AD. It ran from Axmouth, near Exeter, to Lincoln and was built as a front line communications link prior to the conquest by the Romans of the rest of the country. The name 'Stretton' is used for 14 or 15 other settlements in England found close to a Roman road. 'Fosse' derives from the Latin word 'fossa', meaning ditch, and refers to the trench which the Romans dug on either side.

Although we associate straightness with Roman roads, the road through Stretton is somewhat winding. This is almost certainly because the present Fosse Way is not on the original alignment. Although

The Fosse Way at its junction with Brookside.

there is no clear archaeological evidence to prove this, the indications are that the original road was slightly nearer to the centre of the village. Following the Roman occupation, the road may have fallen into disuse, probably becoming nothing more than a rough cart track with no maintenance being carried out for hundreds of years. Coupled with field boundary alterations during medieval times, this has resulted in the route we have today. The location of Frog Hall, an inn dating back to at least the 16th century, also suggests that the Fosse may once have run in a straight line through this point.

A more recent alteration to the route of the Fosse Way was made with the construction of the roundabout on the A45 at the War Memorial, where the approaches to the roundabout diverted the road slightly further to the east.

Locally the Fosse has also been referred to by other names. At the time of the Frog Hall murder (recounted elsewhere in the book), a statement in 1840 by a witness, James Cooper referred to the section of the Fosse at Stretton as Moor Lane. On the map of 1763 the same section is marked as "The Falls."

While many Roman roads lost their significance over the centuries, other roads between developing towns and cities became more important. Heath roads and paths over common land emerged and the enclosure of packages of land created new routes. Some roads were heavily used and the result was the turnpike system under which turnpike trusts developed, maintained and collected tolls from major roads. This reached its peak in the mid 18th century and continued well into the 19th century.

> **A TRAVELLER'S JOURNAL IN 1650 RECORDS -**
>
> *"passing through robbers to Dunchurch, with its towns-folk of plundering and gluttonous fame."*
>
> *"In 1686 one Jonathan Simpson robbed Lord Delamere of 350 guineas, together with 'innumerable drovers, pedlars and market people' along the road and was executed the next year aged thirty two."*

THE LONDON ROAD

One such route was the road which separates the parishes of Stretton and Wolston, which we now know as the A45.

The Dunsmore had remained desolate and sparsely populated for centuries. Until the middle of the 18th century, maps show little more than a track across the heath and with limited habitation, the area developed a bad name as the scene of much highway robbery.

Despite its reputation, however, it was an important route between London and the North West. In the 1700s it was referred to as the Chester Road and was also known as the London-Liverpool and the London-Holyhead Road.

In the mid 18th century, with the growing importance of trade and industry, the road

> *"We would play 'whip and top' on the London Road. We had to be really careful to jump out of the way of the Scammels."*
>
> *"The old cement lorries were a common sight. If we were late for work (in Coventry), we would cycle close to one of these and hold on. If he was a good chap, he would go steady, but if he didn't want you on he would swing you off. If he went ever-so fast you dare not let go."*

> *"One curious feature was the presence of milestones across the Dunsmore which were of a type not found anywhere else - the stones being cut into the shape of two or more steps for the convenience of horsemen."*

became even more important. It was transformed eventually into a turnpike road by the great road builder Thomas Telford. A toll house was located at the top of Knightlow Hill where the London Road entered the parish and there may well have been a further toll house at its other end where it crosses into a different parish.

By this time habitation in Stretton was already growing around coaching houses and inns which offered welcome havens to travellers, particularly as the Dunsmore was still known to be a wild and dangerous place. By the end of the 18th century, a large number of inns and cottages were located along the London Road (see Chapter 12).

At the top of Knightlow Hill, close by the Knightlow Stone, was a collection of five or six houses. These included not only two inns but a forge to provide for the horse-drawn traffic which used the road. There were also buildings on the opposite side of the road. Two shire horses were kept in the stables to assist any vehicles unable to manage the long haul. In fact the hill was once a great deal steeper but its gradient was reduced in the 1950s during work on the dual carriageway.

> *"The weather on the moor was also inhospitable. In 1836 no fewer than seventeen coaches were snowed up on the heath. The development of the London Road as a busy thoroughfare hides its moorland location but even in modern times this story was repeated when in December 1990 a blizzard stranded dozens of cars along the road and left most of the village without electricity for several days."*

The London Road, around 1910, at its junction with School Lane before the dual carriageway was constructed, showing the 'Dun Cow' on the left and the 'Black Dog Inn,' now demolished, on the right.

The London Road at the top of Knightlow Hill with Freeboard Lane on the left.

Two wells and a coal store later supplied vehicles driven by steam engines which passed along the road from the industrial heart of the Midlands. In the 20th century a number of people have vague recollections of an old toll house on the London Road. This was a small cottage, owned by a man called Billy Brooks, situated right on the edge of the old road. The family would supply tea to weary travellers and one person can remember a petrol pump outside.

"In the 1930s the lads used to sit on the monument on a Sunday afternoon, watching for vehicles to come by, and bet a halfpenny on the last figure of the number plate. There were so few vehicles, we would sometimes wait half an hour."

"The road was pretty quiet in the 1930s. I can only remember two residents in Stretton owning cars at this time. Lister-Kaye was one..."

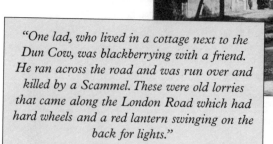

"One lad, who lived in a cottage next to the Dun Cow, was blackberrying with a friend. He ran across the road and was run over and killed by a Scammel. These were old lorries that came along the London Road which had hard wheels and a red lantern swinging on the back for lights."

The London Road passing Frog Hall in the early years of this century.

106

THE AVENUE OF LIME TREES

The original avenue which now forms part of the A45 did not in fact consist of the lime trees we see today but of elms and firs, planted in 1740 by the second Duke of Montagu. Some of the firs still remain near Dunchurch. His vision of a great avenue stretching as far as London earned him the name 'John the Planter.' His dreams of tree planting were not limited to Warwickshire and he was eventually curtailed by the lack of permission to cross land belonging to other powerful men. He died before he could complete his vision of "The Long Avenue", which stopped at Dunchurch. Around 1912 a great storm destroyed a large number of the original trees which were then replaced by limes during the First World War. According to the Reverend Squires' notes, these were planted to the memory of men of the 29th Division.

> *"Such was the imagination of 'John the Planter' that Sarah, the famous Duchess of Marlborough, is reported to have said of him that he did all the things expected of a 15-year old boy, except that he was 52 years of age. However, the remark may have been coloured by the fact that she was his mother-in-law."*

The unveiling of the War Memorial, erected in memory of the 29th Division on 24th May 1921.

THE WAR MEMORIAL

The inscription reads: *"Here in the centre of England, where Telford's coaching road from London to Holyhead is crossed by the Roman Fosse Way, on the 12th of March 1915 His Majesty King George V reviewed his troops of the Immortal 29th Division shortly before they embarked for active service in Gallipoli. In memory of their stay in Warwickshire 1914-15 and of their incomparable service since, the Avenue on this road was replanted and this monument erected by the inhabitants of the County."*

The road became a dual carriageway in the late 1950s, resulting in the demolition of a number of cottages and houses which stood opposite Frog Hall and the Dun Cow. The most notable of these was the Black Dog Inn, to which reference is made in another chapter of the book.

In 1983 an increasing list of fatal traffic accidents at the junction of the London Road and the Fosse Way led to two parish councillors, Jesse Quinney and Ian Smith, erecting their own blackspot warning sign at the crossroads after fruitless appeals to the local traffic authority for more than seven years. In 1984 their efforts paid off and a large island was built at a cost of £350,000 to produce a slower but safer flow of traffic along both major roads.

A further move by the Department of Transport in 1994 led to the closure of the central reservation in the dual carriageway by the Dun Cow, where 13 accidents had been recorded since 1986. Sadly, this also divided the ancient lane between Wolston and Stretton.

THE OXFORD ROAD

The modern A423 follows an ancient way between Oxford and Coventry known locally as the Oxford Road. This formed a major route for the movement of people and armies and for the transport of goods (see Chapter 10). The 1704 enclosure agreement for Stretton specifies that it should remain as marked and be thirty yards wide, slightly narrower than the forty yards specified for the old London Road.

FINACRE LANE

This is referred to as 'Finiker Way' in 1763. The origin of the name possibly means the end of a plot of land, rather than Fine Acre as the modern variation would suggest.

(Fin meaning 'end')

On the 1763 map, the Oxford Road is marked as a turnpike or toll road. The toll gate is shown at the top of what was then known as 'Finiker Way,' now Finacre Lane.

FREEBOARD LANE

The name of the ancient way now known as Freeboard Lane originates from times when communication was far less easy than in modern times. In the eighteenth century the lane was known as Free-born Lane, thought to be a corruption of 'fire-born'. Both good and bad news was announced by a system of beacons across the land and the local beacon, one of a chain reaching from High Cross to the keep at Warwick Castle, was situated at the top of Knightlow Hill. On the 1763 map this is also marked as Stretton Lane and what we now know as Plott Lane is named the Coventry Road. The section of the lane close to the London Road was also once called Robinson's Lane, relating to a family living in the Plott Cottages.

LANES AND FOOTPATHS

The present pattern of lanes and footpaths generally follow those agreed at the time of the enclosure agreement for Stretton in 1704. These would have been maintained over the centuries under the clause requiring that "all ancient footways should lie as they formerly did before the enclosure of the common and open fields of Stretton" and that "the public roads and cartways shall be repaired, mended and kept in repair at the public charge of the parties hereunto, their heirs and assigns [successors]." This was achieved by means of a levy paid by the landowners.

The majority of the paths and lanes covered by the agreement were ancient ways linking village to village and included the three major thoroughfares already described. One of the oldest paths listed was the route between the churches of Wolston and Stretton (today School Lane). Frankton Lane and Rugby Lane still follow approximately the same route, although a bridle path can be seen near the top end of Rugby Lane which may have been part of an earlier way.

With the creation of packages of land, new ways were also specified in 1704 between and around plots and fields. Some of the more notable lanes are mentioned here.

COFFIN WALK

The name of the path between Stretton and Princethorpe originates from the need for a passage for coffins to the respective Church of England and Catholic graveyards in the two villages. An ancient bylaw required the path to be kept five feet wide to allow a horse-drawn vehicle to be used along the route. On early maps the footpath is shown running from the church to the Fosse about halfway to Princethorpe and did not continue in a direct line at that time.

CUT THROAT LANE

The path runs alongside 'The Castle' across to Coffin Walk and was called this after a local man committed suicide by cutting his own throat.

KAYSBROOK DRIVE

Built in late 20th century, the drive was named after Jane Kaysbrook, the wife of Daniel Parrott, a local builder who did much for the village around the late 19th century. The timbered Parrott's house originally stood on this site.

SCHOOL LANE

This ancient route was named School Lane in relatively recent times because of the location of the old school at the junction with Plott Lane. It was formerly called Dog Lane, possibly because of the dog-leg half way down or because it led to the Black Dog -which served the community as a very significant inn and meeting place - at the junction of the lane with the London Road. It formed part of the old path to Wolston church.

The A45 London Road before the roundabout was built.

BARTLETTS HILL

When he was a lad, a Mr Bartlett learned to ride his bike on the hill. So memorable was the achievement that the name stuck.

BURNTHURST LANE

This long-established route links the village with the outlying settlement of Burnthurst. This hamlet which is within Stretton Parish was originally at the edge of the Forest of Arden. The word 'hurst' meaning wood, the name Burnthurst implies that the area was probably cleared from the forest many centuries ago, using fire. The lane has certainly existed since the field enclosures but is probably much older.

12

THE VILLAGE INNS
HOSTELRIES, ALEHOUSES AND PUBS

Like many villages, Stretton on Dunsmore had its fair share of inns, hostelries, ale houses and public houses over the centuries which provided both refreshment and a focus of community life.

In the centre of the village, the two major public houses remain to this day.

The Shoulder of Mutton in the early years of this century.

THE SHOULDER OF MUTTON

The 'Shoulder' is the oldest public house in the village and is a free house (not tied to a brewery). Deeds of the pub dated 1757 show the main building and five cottages. Three of these stood in a row with their back to the Church in the modern car park area but were demolished in the middle of this century. One remaining cottage is now known as Rose Cottage and the fifth also remains as a two-storey building facing the main building. This is now used for storage but was originally used as a 'cellar' and club room, with a large room on the first floor which provided the venue for many social occasions. The main building had no real cellar because of flooding from the brook. Until the mid 20th century, beer had to be supplied from the opposite building with pipes running below the path.

In the 19th century the pub was run by a victualler, Richard Allinstone, who combined the premises with his other trade, that of a butcher. It was rebuilt in 1820. In 1949 the main building was rebuilt again after a visiting air rifle team backed their van into a supporting wall. The wall collapsed and, because the house was a veritable rabbit warren of small rooms, it was decided to redesign the layout. At the height of post-war austerity, much of the original fixtures and fittings were re-used, together with other recycled material from elsewhere. The Minton floor tiles, now hidden below stone slabs since its refurbishment in 1997, were brought from an old Coventry building and bore such a complex pattern that it took two men a fortnight to lay them.

**MEMORIES FROM
'THE MUTTON'**

"It stayed the same for years. It was like going into a general store where the proprietor has to be summoned from the back room. The big event was the 'Alterations' in 1949."

"It was an ale house of the old school. As I walked in, every pair of eyes in the place turned on me. I was a stranger."

"The main bar was furnished with the sort of furniture you might find in the station buffet in the film 'Brief Encounter', except there was a baby grand piano in the corner on which Mrs Whitby gave music lessons."

"I remember an incident when the landlady used to cook on the open hearth of the parlour. Some of the locals decided to lift the lid of a pie and eat the contents. Terrified of being discovered before they left, they filled it with cinders. The scallywags fled but the consternation at the publican's table will long be remembered!"

"Men used to come in from the fields with their lunch and sit there with their dinner and a pint. No-one minded them bringing their own food. It was the way of things."

"Many an important meeting was held in the little room. The electric heater would be switched on, a round of drinks got in. Usually the landlord put the kettle on as well and served tea and biscuits."

"I have a nice old boy who comes in and plays the top ten of 1913. I enjoy living in 1950. If I get any skinheads in, I just play Mantovani on the gramophone." (Paul Whitby, 1996)

Most modern memories of the pub are linked to the family who ran the business from 1914 when James Underhill took over the premises. On his death his wife, Ruth, took over the licence, followed by her son-in-law, Frederick Whitby. He was succeeded by his wife Emma and later his son Paul. Emma's discipline has become legendary but, although strict, she was held in great respect, both as a landlady and as a piano teacher.

Many aspects of social life have been associated with the 'Shoulder.' In 1776 the first Friendly Society meeting was held here (see Chapter 6) and it has been the venue for meetings of many other clubs and societies. Until 1921 the two-storey building opposite the main building was used as the Village Hall.

Like many pubs, it also provided a venue not just for meetings but for activities and competitive games. The most prominent activity was the Rifle Club which still exists today. At the turn of the century all the local pubs in the Rugby area had a rifle club (indoor shooting) but only three clubs remain. The Stretton Club started in the early 1900s, established itself at the Shoulder of Mutton after the First World War and won numerous trophies and awards. Darts, dominoes, cribbage and whist were regularly played in 'the snug' as late as the 1980s.

On the death of his mother, Paul Whitby assumed the role of landlord. The pub became a social centre and offered a venue for numerous events, including jazz evenings, small parties and a wider range of committee meetings. A new era and a cheery welcome produced many happy memories for local residents and also attracted customers from further afield. The beer also achieved acclaim in the 'CAMRA Good Beer Guide'. After a lifetime at the pub, however, Paul eventually moved to other ventures and a new home in Church Hill.

In 1997 the pub passed to new owners who modernised the old interior and added a restaurant to its facilities.

THE OAK AND BLACK DOG

The 18th century map does not show a pub on this site but its buildings date back some 300 years in the form of a row of cottages. Photographs from around 1900 show it in its present form.

The Oak & Black Dog pub was once just cottages in terrace.

The name of the pub is almost certainly unique, being a combination of the names of two pubs. As verified by a number of maps and by previous licensees, the two were never adjacent but the name 'Black Dog' was incorporated when the old pub of this name on the London Road was demolished.

"The Oak", as it is commonly called by locals, remains a traditional pub used by farming communities, with a character quite different from that of the 'Shoulder.' It also supported a number of activities over the centuries, including a darts club, shooting club and a skittle alley in the 1930s. For many years it acted as the headquarters of the Stretton Football Club and the Friendly Society (see Chapter 6). In modern times it is regularly used as a centre for meetings and functions. Bar meals and a variety of social events make it an attraction to both residents and visitors.

The Oak is also the focal point for the Duck Race (see Chapter 14). Plastic ducks are 'sold' and raced with great merriment to a point a short way downstream. Money raised has been donated to a variety of charities and amounts to many thousands of pounds.

The many establishments which served travellers along the old London to Holyhead Road (the A45) are now long gone but eight inns are clearly shown on old maps of the parish.

MEMORIES FROM THE 'OAK'

"The rooms were very small in the 1930s and there was a shooting range upstairs."

"The Sunday Mercury 1954 tells of the landlord at that time, Mr Dawson, being a retired jockey who won many races, including the Two Thousand Guineas, and rode for the Rothchilds. Sadly his career ended in 1926 when he broke 'almost every bone in his body' in a crash at Beecher's Brook in the Grand National."

Did you know that relatives of Kevin McGhee (previous landlord at the Oak) ran the rival Mutton in the 19th century?

THE DUN COW

There is no sign of the Dun Cow on Henry Beighton's map of 1725 but a church register entry in 1731 refers to a stranger 'who died at ye old Dun Cow'. A pub of that name did exist on the London Road around that time but not on the modern site. The map dated 1763 clearly shows that there were no buildings on the modern day site at the top of Wolston Lane and it locates the Dun Cow at the top of Knightlow Hill in the cluster of buildings which still exist today. The new site is recorded in the 19th century and the name existed until the mid 1990s when it became a restaurant (Stretton Place) and then a club (named first the Oasis and then Crazy Daisy's). The current building replaced an older one located slightly further back from the present road. This was demolished approximately 70 years ago.

MEMORIES FROM THE DUN COW

"The top tower of All Saints Church was dead in line with the keyhole of the front door of the Old Dun Cow. A higher power than the landlord was keeping watch."

"The pub was a very 'lively' meeting place. Young girls could freely go to most places around the village - apart from the Old Dun Cow. It was so popular that coaches would arrive from Birmingham and Leicester."

"If the doors were still on at 10 o'clock they had had a very quiet night. You could always have a good scrap up there if you felt like one."

"When it became a night club in the 1990s, the teenagers in the village thought heaven had come."

"Pantomime rehearsals in the night club room were well-oiled but the lights were so dim you couldn't read the script."

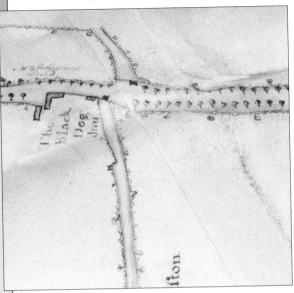

London Road at School Lane junction (from 1763 map)

The Dun Cow, London Road.

115

The old Dun Cow with the new Dun Cow under construction on the left.

THE BLACK DOG

In Dugdale's History of Warwickshire (circa 1605-1686), the Black Dog Inn is mentioned as the location for the Petty Sessions for the Knightlow Hundred (one of the four divisions of the county). The local court and appeals to the Commissioners for taxes were held here. It was an important building not just for this purpose. In the late 18th and early 19th century the trustees of Stretton Charities held their meetings here and on 28th November 1838, the first receiving house for mail in the Stretton area was established at the inn. The name may be attributed to the 'Black Dog of Arden', a favourite of Edward II in the 14th century. Piers Gaveston became known by this derogatory name because of his confrontations with Guy of Warwick, regarded as a local hero of the time.

In his notes on the history of the village, the Reverend Squires believed that the Black Dog was also later known as Knightlow House which stood opposite the modern Dun Cow (now Crazy Daisy's Night Club). When the dual carriageway was built, this building was demolished but some of the original outhouses still exist and have been restored as cottages.

"There were a lot of activities at the pubs. One used to host the flower and vegetable show."

"I had four sisters but they were never allowed in a pub. Women came down from the north to the factories during the war - they were a bit more brazen and used to go in. You didn't see women smoke either until this time. The 'Yanks' were responsible."

THE RED LION

An inn is shown on the 1763 map which shared the site with the old Dun Cow. The innkeeper was listed as Edward Tirral. A building alongside was described as being 'a look-out' for the road. As a toll house was also situated in this group of cottages, the trade from travellers at the top of the hill would have been significant.

FROG HALL

There is evidence that Frog Hall was built around 1535. With the later increase in the coaching trade between London and the North, the original small cottage was extended with a new large building and stables and outbuildings added. It became a major coaching inn known as the Frog Inn and also the Frogge and Phoenix. An early newspaper article suggests it derived its name from the innumerable frogs found in a pit on its land. In the 18th century it became the meeting place for Justices of the Peace where the overseers of the parish of Rugby and the vicinity brought their accounts for inspection. For some years it was also the venue for the Wroth Silver breakfast. There are indications that the Fosse Way may have passed nearer to its doors than at present, thus making it convenient for both travellers along the Fosse and along the London to Liverpool Road. However, no change in the course of the Fosse is shown on the 1763 map.

"The Quarter Sessions records for 1696 lists Francis Wright, a victualler, fined for keeping a disorderly alehouse and 'allowing drink in his house at the time of divine service for several Sundays after another. Also for keeping a greyhound without qualification and for 'tracing' hares in the snow."

In addition to the many inns, ale houses were also located in various cottages along the London Road, at the top of Knightlow Hill and in the village. These were little more than cottages where people gathered to drink ale. They did not provide food and accommodation. One such ale house, known as Dudley's beer shop, was located opposite Frog Hall in a row of buildings demolished during the building of the dual carriageway. This is mentioned in the evidence given for the Frog Hall murder around 1836 (see Chapter 4).

The 1763 map also shows four other inns along the London Road and within the parish boundary:

THE WHITE LION

The White Lion was on the north side of the London Road but this was not marked as an inn on the Ordnance Survey map of 1834-40. The filling station and site of Bob's Café are in approximately the same location.

THE GEORGE

This inn was on the south side of the London Road to the east of the Fosse and opposite the White Lion. On Ordnance Survey maps between 1834-40 this was still shown as an inn but was not recorded in 1886.

THE WHEATSHEAF

The Wheatsheaf is shown as an inn on the north side of the London Road, approximately a quarter of a mile to the east of its junction with Rugby Lane. On the 1834-40 Ordnance Survey maps this is not shown as an inn.

COLD COMFORT INN

This inn is shown at the far eastern boundary of the parish on the north side of the London Road. This is later referred to as Cold Comfort Farm.

> "There were quite a lot of 'off-sales' from the pubs. Children could come and collect these. They would bring their dad's bottle and we would fill them and seal them with a special paper seal. My mother didn't like licking these seals for some reason and used to dip them in the beer instead. You had to have a sealed bottle when you walked out."

The Dun Cow when newly built in the early 1930s.

13

CUSTOMS AND FOLKLORE
TRADITIONS FROM THE PAST, FESTIVALS OF THE PRESENT

L ike every other village, Stretton has its own customs which are important to the continuity of the community. Unlike other villages, we are able to boast a ceremony which has been observed for many centuries. This chapter deals with both ancient and modern traditions, legends and celebrations.

WROTH SILVER

The collection of Wroth Silver dates back over eight hundred years to the twelfth century, offering us a living link with the Middle Ages. The ceremony has been held on Knightlow Hill on November 11th almost continuously since that time. Representatives of villages in the area pay their dues to the Lord of the Manor and retire to a local hostelry for breakfast, speeches and poetry reading. A study of the ceremony reveals fascinating details of the history of our area and of the changes that have taken place during that period.

19th century photograph of the Wroth Silver representatives paying their dues.

The origin of the ceremony

Opinions differ as to the original purpose of the ceremony. It might have been a form of tax paid to the local lord for making use of 'wasteland' in the area. (A similar custom is still observed in the New Forest where 'Wrather money' is paid by Forest tenants to the lord of the manor in return for the right to graze cattle and pigs on the land.) Until recently it was thought most likely that Wroth Silver was paid for the right to move cattle along the old drove roads in the area - a sort of mediaeval road fund licence - and that the term 'Wroth' was a derivation of the Saxon term 'word' meaning a road. However, the latest research suggests that the local freemen were obliged to pay in order to provide a baggage train for the King when he travelled in the area. Dating the start of the ceremony is not easy but there are a number of clues. The villages concerned are all in the hundred of Knightlow - one of the four divisions of the county of Warwickshire at that time. This hundred is first described in 1169 as 'Cnuchtelawa.' At the time of the Domesday survey in 1086 Stretton was in the smaller hundred of Marton. Around half of the villages involved in the ceremony were then in the adjacent hundreds of Stoneleigh or Brinklow. So it seems most likely that the ceremony in its current form began during the twelfth century when the administrative division of Knightlow was established from the amalgamation of these three hundreds.

The first written record of the collection of Wroth Silver is in 1210, when it amounted to 14s ¹/₂d, a handsome sum at that time; however, it may have been established earlier than this. Payment was originally made to the King and in 1275 Richard of Stretton paid £29.17s in taxes from this hundred: this sum would have been the product of several different taxes including Wroth Silver, fishing and head tax (an early form of poll tax). Lordship of the Hundred (and hence the right to collect these taxes) remained with the crown until 1629 when it was purchased for £40 by Sir Francis Leigh whose ancestors owned Stoneleigh Abbey. His descendants included Lord John Scott whose statue still stands in Dunchurch. For the past 140 years it has belonged to the Dukes of Buccleuch and Queensberry. The present holder is the 9th Duke of Buccleuch.

Size of contribution

The amounts paid by the twenty-five villages today still relate to their size in the Middle Ages and add up to 9s 4¹/₂d (46p). A group of nine villages used to contribute but opted out of payment sometime after 1730; these included Rugby, which used to pay less than Stretton since in 1086 Stretton was larger than Rugby or Birmingham. Amounts were decimalised in 1971 but not adjusted to modern equivalents in cost. The largest contributors, Harbury, Long Itchington and Leamington Hastings, were all well-established places in the Domesday survey, with a sizeable acreage and population, large numbers of ploughs and at least one priest (and therefore presumably a church). Some places such as Bubbenhall were more important in terms of Wroth Silver and other places such as Napton were less important. This evidence suggests that the contributions reflect the pattern of settlement during the Middle Ages.

Forfeit - a red nose!

Non-payment of the appropriate sum incurs a fine - the village concerned is required to pay 100 pence for every penny owing or to produce a white bull with red ears and red nose. Until recently it was thought to be because Dunsmore Heath - along with other parts of the British Isles - used to be home to a breed of wild white cows with 'red' markings. This could also relate to the local pub name of the 'Dun Cow'. Herds of similar cattle still exist, and are

WROTH SILVER CONTRIBUTIONS:	
¹/₂p	Arley, Astley, Birdingbury, Bramcote, Shilton & Barnacle, Little Walton, Woolscott, Bourton & Draycote, Napton, Radford Semele, Whitley
1p	Bubbenhall, Churchover, Ladbrooke, Princethorpe, Stretton on Dunsmore, Toft (once part of Dunchurch), Weston under Wetherley
1¹/₂p	Hillmorton, Hopsford, Wolston & Marston, Lillington, Leamington Hastings
11p	Long Itchington
11¹/₂p	Harbury

apparently very fierce, so catching the forfeit would have been quite a penalty. The last time one was offered in lieu of payment was around 1800 but it was rejected as not being the right colour. However, recent research suggests that the bull forfeit could be an invention of the second Duke of Montagu - known for his love of hoaxes - who may have introduced this to spice up the ceremony in 1729. Be that as it may, a handsome statue of such a bull now takes pride of place on the breakfast table.

The Wroth Silver representatives breakfast at the Dun Cow, London Road, in 1899.

Location of the ceremony

The ceremony is carried out on the summit of Knightlow Hill close to the boundary with the parish of Ryton, around the base of an old stone cross that stands on a mound there. Sadly the actual 'cross' has disappeared although this has the advantage that the hole where the shaft once fitted makes a useful receptacle for the pennies. The date of the cross is not known accurately (estimates range from 'Saxon' through to fourteenth century) but it may have been a wayside 'praying cross'. The mound may mark the site of an even older burial place and could have been the site of a Saxon 'Thing': the equivalent of the local County Council meeting. There used to be four pine trees around the mound, placed there in 1740 by 'John the Planter' (see Chapter 11). The date when the shaft and cross were removed is not known. Knightlow cross is drawn as a cross on old maps of the area from 1695 to 1840. However, it was described by Dugdale in 1730 as 'the cross sometime there' which indicates it has already disappeared. It stands on a high point, overlooking the Coventry basin, and would have been a useful feature for travellers in the days before compasses and ordnance survey maps. All the villages contributing Wroth Silver are sited within 12 miles of the cross.

During the nineteenth century, and probably much earlier, the breakfast after the ceremony was held in the 'Frogge and Phoenix', a sixteenth century coaching inn located further along the London Road (known today as 'Frog Hall'). In the 1880s it moved to the 'Dun Cow' on the A45 (now 'Crazy Daisy's' night-club) where it remained for a hundred years until 1988. Since then it has been

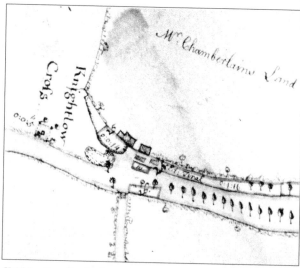

Knightlow Cross, London Road, where the Wroth Silver ceremony takes place.

held at a number of establishments in the vicinity and in the last few years at the Old Bull and Butcher on the Banbury Road. It seems likely that the original location would have been the nearest place to eat from the Knightlow Cross, especially in the days before the car or the bicycle.

The time of the ceremony

Martinmas - the feast of St Martin - was a quarter day at the end of the agricultural year when accounts for the year would be settled. The timing before sunrise is unusual and must have been extremely inconvenient for the further-flung villages. The ceremony traditionally takes place on Martinmas Eve and this harks back to the time when the new day began when the sun rose and not at midnight (Martinmas Eve is in fact November 10th and not November 11th).

Details of the ceremony

The field is the only local piece of land still owned in the vicinity by the Duke. The tenant farmer is still paid 1 shilling (5p) to clean out the base of the cross beforehand, ready for the ceremony. For many years Bill Quarterman, who lived in a nearby cottage, did this, like his father before him; he also used to be given pennies by local farmers to mind their horses during the ceremony. The current tenant, Richard Postlethwaite, lives in Wolston. An advertisement appears in a local newspaper for the "Annual Audit for receiving the Wroth Silver due" inviting all from whom payments are due to attend at 6.45am. The ceremony is also open to observers. It starts before the sun rises with a speech from the Duke's agent, facing east. Originally contributors would have circled the stone three times, perhaps to bring good fortune for the coming year, but this is not the custom nowadays. Others may substitute the payment for absentee villages. Attendance during the 20th century has reached over 300 on occasion, though it dropped to 6 at one point during the Second World War. The longest attending person at present is David Eadon, who has been going for over 60 years, having first attended as a child; he has written a fascinating booklet about the ceremony along with William Waddilove.

Originally contributors were invited to breakfast afterwards by the Steward. Nowadays this has become a pre-paid, all ticket affair.

Since 1952 a tradition has grown up of a local person reciting a poem written especially for the occasion. Examples of some of these poems can be read in the 'Wroth Silver Today' booklet. The ceremony has been broadcast on radio and television, and recorded on audiotape and video.

A PERSONAL ACCOUNT OF THE CEREMONY

"I woke early from excitement, got up at 6, dressed warmly and scraped ice off the car. I parked on the verge of Freeboard Lane, full of shadowy figures and cars. We crossed the A45 and walked over the frosted grass and dead leaves to join the group already forming around the Knightlow cross. A circle of canes kept back spectators and helped us all to see. Last night's half-moon hung ghostly in the sky, whilst the new day was dawning in the East. There was an air of suppressed excitement and hugs for old friends. The Lady Mayoress erupted on the scene in her scarlet robes and golden chain of office. The Duke's agent proclaimed the time-honoured words, drowning the traffic, as the ceremony proceeded. Each village in turn was called and one or more of those present threw a coin in the stone, murmuring "Wroth Silver". There were "oohs" when the larger amounts were called (elevenpence halfpenny for Harbury!). I cast my modest penny for Stretton. A fiery glow was spreading in the east and a parley of rooks flapped by overhead, off to find their first meal of the day. In five minutes the ceremony was over. We repaired to the Old Bull and Butcher where breakfast was laid out in their airy new conservatory, a magical place to sit facing east and watch the sun rise. We ate a hearty English breakfast, surrounded by photographs of previous ceremonies. After the meal we drank toasts to the Queen and the Duke of Buccleuch and Queensberry, in rum and hot milk, and were given permission to smoke tobacco in clay pipes laid out by each place. I made my first ever, rather unsuccessful attempt at smoking. The Duke's agent Mr Wordie gave an entertaining speech and welcomed the colts - us newcomers. The Lady Mayoress responded, reminding us that on this particular day we were commemorating the First World War 80 years ago, as well as 800 years of Wroth Silver. David Eadon recounted some of the fascinating history of the ceremony and Peter Miller read a splendid poem 'Exceeding Wroth' he had composed for the occasion. By 9 o'clock it was all over and I set off for work, glowing with warmth from the company, the food and the rum."

Unanswered questions

It is tantalising to speculate about the collection of Wroth Silver. When exactly did it start and what was it for? Why are some villages in Knightlow not 'called' and what is the explanation for the surprising exceptions such as Ryton and Church Lawford close by, and important places like Southam further away? Why have the amounts stayed the same over the centuries? When did the reducing value of the collection make its original tax-gathering purpose meaningless? There are reports of grumbling and cursing from participants in 1722, and we know that contributions ceased to be compulsory in 1800; who resurrected the ceremony fifteen years later? Maybe it adds to the attraction that we do not know all the answers. We can wonder at this mysterious link with our past, and join with other local parishes in performing what is thought to be Britain's oldest ceremony.

THE TOMB OF THE DANISH GIANT

"The site of the Knightlow Cross has caused much speculation. A 19th century historian believed that a Danish giant, who was slain by Guy Earl of Warwick in AD92, lies buried in the Knightlow tumulus and that local tradition fixed the scene of this combat on the borders of Saxon and Danish territory, which was divided roughly by Watling Street."

White cattle which used to roam the Dunsmore are still bred near the town of Warwick.

THE LEGEND OF THE DUN COW

The name 'Dun Cow' has been used for a number of inns in the district and is taken from local legend and tales dating back as far as the 12th century.

The earliest mention of the legend is by a Dr Caius in 1570 who described relics of a monster animal displayed at Warwick Castle. A detailed version of the story is found in an account by John Shirley in 1703 and tells of a 'dreadful and monstrous beast in the likeness of a cow' which terrified the people of the Dunsmore and destroyed their cattle. It was said to be six yards long and was a dun colour with red, fiery eyes. After King Athelstan had offered a knighthood and gifts to anyone who could slay the beast, Guy of Warwick is said to have cornered and killed her in a thicket of trees on the Dunsmore. By tradition this was close to an inn known as the Blue Boar, where, according to the Rev. W.O. Watt, in 1893, the soil remains black and indelibly stained by the animal's blood. (The Blue Boar appears on 19th century maps of the area).

HARVEST FESTIVAL

A thanksgiving service for harvest has long been a tradition in agricultural communities throughout the world. Stretton was no exception and continues the tradition to this day. This is recorded in many examples:

The Parish magazine in October 1914 refers to the Harvest Thanksgiving Festival for a plentiful harvest gathered in perfect weather. Despite being cushioned from the war in Europe, the village was well aware of the suffering of the First World War and proceeds were given to the Belgian Relief Fund.

> *"Harvest Festival was always a favourite. It usually happened that the people who provided the fruit and vegetables and did all the decorating were the ones who turned out on Monday night to buy them back again."*

After the First World War, life returned to normal and the magazine for October 1922 records "a great Thanksgiving Service" at harvest time.

In the earlier part of the century, a baker's basket from the Wilcox bakery would stand on the altar steps of the church, together with a large loaf in the shape of a sheaf of corn.

In October 1973 the Pendulum refers to the produce from the harvest festival being distributed to the sick. This is also a longstanding tradition and over the years has taken the form of distribution to hospitals, the sick and the elderly. On many occasions a sale of produce has also been organised, with the money raised distributed appropriately.

In 1971 the Stretton Wives Fellowship, renamed the Ladies Fellowship in later years, revived the tradition of a harvest supper. This is normally held on the first Saturday of October. Approaching the Millennium, the supper is still prepared by the members of the Fellowship, who remember numerous happy occasions over the years. Despite occasional 'experiments', today's menu has changed little from the traditional rural fare - cold meats, salads, jacket potatoes, apple pie and cream, cheese and biscuits and coffee. From humble beginnings, the event now raises almost £300 which is donated to a variety of charities, both locally and overseas.

In the parish magazine for October 1922 a reference is also made to the celebration of All Saints Day on November 1st with a special communion service and the annual social to be held on the evening before (All Hallow E'en).

MAYPOLE DANCING

Maypole Day was the high spot in the village year and everyone joined in. This is well recorded this century but is a tradition dating back many hundreds of years as a celebration of spring on May 1st (May Day). In the 20th century this was organised by the school, with the teacher choosing a girl aged 13 or 14 to become May Queen. In the early part of the century, each farmer would lend a horse and cart which would be decorated as a 'float' by the mothers. One float would have a piano on it. Collections were made which went towards the cost of a party held afterwards in the Village Hall.

The last May celebration before the Second World War was a more conservative affair.

MAY DAY

"We would start in the centre of the village and process up to Lister-Kaye's, the Manor, where we would receive sweets. We would then move on to the Dun Cow where we would receive a packet of crisps and a bottle of pop. Next we called at Wolston Grange where Captain and Mrs Stiff gave us lemonade.
The policeman would have the day off duty but would ride round in his uniform, stopping lorries and encouraging them to put a donation in the box."

May Day in Stretton on Dunsmore in 1906.

Maypole dancing in 1947.

The May Queen (Kath Edwards) walked down into the village from school. A group of 10 or so attendants were intended to accompany her but, due to an outbreak of chickenpox and pouring rain, the numbers were depleted.

The celebration continued after the war but disappeared for a number of years. It was eventually revived when June Edmans, a former pupil at Stretton herself, once again began to teach the new generation of children the traditional dances to strains of "Coming 'Round the Rye". The event was held for some years in the school playground but the procession was revived in 1993 and on a Sunday in early May, the procession of the chosen Queen, King and attendants still makes its way from the school to the Village Green where children dance around the maypole in the time-honoured fashion.

VILLAGE FETES AND FESTIVALS

Living memories of village fetes locate them not only on the Village Green but also in the Pool Yard (land between the Church and the Shoulder of Mutton) and on the Knob (land at

On 21 June 1887 the village celebrated Queen Victoria's Jubilee in grand manner. A thanksgiving service was held at the Church, followed by a feast for all above fifteen years old on tables extending for some distance in the centre of the village. This consisted of cold joints of roast and boiled beef, veal and mutton with new potatoes, radishes, cucumber and cheese. Afterwards hot plum pudding with brandy dip accompanied by ale and nectar.

This was followed by sports, the most interesting being a competition of housewives trundling mops, an obstacle race and the women's race. The latter was won by the poorest woman in the parish who won the prize of half a crown for her large family.

Dancing to the strains of an excellent band was a treat to all until 9.30 pm when Chinese lanterns were hung across the Green and coloured fireworks let off. The day closed with the lighting of two large bonfires - one near the village and one at Knightlow Cross."

'Bowling for a Pig' on the village green at the annual fete in the 1930s.

"A marvellous tea would be prepared in the Village Hall and the children would perform again when the men returned from work at about 6 o'clock. A dance would take place in the evening but the children were only allowed to stay until 8 o'clock."

"It was so exciting that on one occasion, a little girl was left behind. She was immediately balanced on the cross bar of a bicycle by a kind onlooker who peddled after the procession and deposited her on the cart."

the top of Knob Hill). When the house at the Knob was built by the Wilcox family in 1911, fetes and shows were still held in the garden of the new house. Photographs also show evidence of a fancy dress pageant and a party for the troops just after the First World War.

There are also memories of a Church Fete, which included bowling for a real pig. At the Millennium the Village Fete is still a well-established tradition and has been joined by the Church Bazaar at Christmas and the School Fete in June.

The Stretton on Dunsmore May Queen at Wolston Grange in the 1930s.

How the Maypole music was made in 1947.

The first Village Hall fete was organised by the Entertainment Committee. The fete was held on 5 August, 1920 in Mr Faulkner's field. The Dunchurch Band were in attendance with dancing in the field from 7pm and in the Village Hall from 9pm, admittance to be 1 shilling. A full programme of adult and children's races took place together with a tug-of-war competition and sideshows. £75 15s 8d was raised towards the hall fund.

The details of the annual fete in the 1950s, usually held on Whit-Monday, are almost identical to the present day with similar stalls and maypole dancing by the school children of the village. There were often dances in the evening, mainly to the accompaniment of the Southam Works Band.

In 1957 the Reverend Squires introduced a "Church Week" held annually in June, the objects of which were to develop the parish socially and spiritually and raise funds for church maintenance. The church was decorated with flowers and various events were held. The custom survived until 1970.

In 1977 the present Queen's Silver Jubilee was marked with a day of sports, fancy dress competitions, a children's party on the Green and barbecue in the evening and a Millennium fete is planned for the year 2000.

In the 1990s, village fetes continue in traditional manner, often with a theme, such as the Olympics or the World Cup. The proceeds still help to maintain the Village Hall for the general use of the whole community (see Chapter 14).

NOTEWORTHY FETES

"In 1926 the fete was cancelled because of the general strike."

"The presence of a police constable was felt necessary in case of 'bad behaviour' at the dance held in 1928."

"The Whit-Monday dance held in 1934 also produced complaints about the behaviour of certain boys. After due consideration, it was felt that the only way to stop a repetition of such behaviour was to prosecute one boy and ban two others from the hall for a year."

"Dan and Doris Archer were invited to open the fete held summer 1955."

"One intriguing item was the 'Ankle Competition'. Mrs Goodgame, the judge, awarded a pair of silk stockings to the lady with the most attractive ankles."

Fancy dress at a school fete at the bottom of School Lane in the 1950s. Percy Edmans dressed as a school master. The cottages in the background, now demolished, stood on the 'Hillies'.

The planting of the Lime Tree on the green in 1887.

14

VILLAGERS AT LEISURE
CLUBS, GROUPS AND SOCIETIES

Prior to the 20th century leisure time was much restricted by the long hours of work which most adults and children in agricultural communities endured. Traditional festivals connected with the church and with the seasons provided the only regular periods of recreation. In the late 19th century, however, working hours became shorter and bank holidays were generally acknowledged in the 1870s. The public looked towards a greater variety of leisure activities and Stretton was no exception. By the 20th century it had become, and remains, a very socially active community.

Stretton 'Tug o' War' team, 1913.

Shoulder of Mutton Rifle Club 1934-35

"Such was the importance of the new facility that an official opening of the Village Hall was held at a fete on Whit-Monday 1921. Admiral Rose attended to perform the opening ceremony. The Dunchurch Band were engaged, the sports and tea committees leapt into action and a marquee hired at a cost of £3. There was a Punch & Judy show, a sweepstake, balloon stall and 'Mrs Twist and Mrs Kincaid Lennox kindly sold cigarettes.'"

THE VILLAGE HALL

Until the 20th century, meetings were held in a variety of locations, primarily the local inns or the vicarage (Stretton House).

At the end of the First World War a memorial fund was established to commemorate those who died in the First World War. £75 of the fund was allocated to a memorial tablet in the Church, £6 1s 9d (£6.09p) was paid to the church for 'faculty and fees' and the remaining £29 14s 3d (£29.71p) was designated as the 'Village Hall Fund' for the erection of a community building.

> "At the committee meeting, held 2 April, 1940, it was decided to hold a Whit-Monday dance in aid of winter comforts for the troops. £9 was raised and this was added to £1 2s 8d already in the soldiers' parcel fund, sending gifts to all Stretton men in the forces."

A piece of ground, which had previously been used as gardens for the cottages opposite, was donated by the Admiral Rose Estate, subject to the memorial fund committee paying the costs; the building itself was a converted army hut. On Friday, 26 July 1920 the chairman of the Parish Council, L Lister-Kaye, reported that the erection of the hall was complete and the first Trustees, L Lister-Kaye, C L Stiff, T Meredith, T Borsley, H Harvey, H Paget, C Howkins and W Wilcox, were elected.

> "The field in Rugby Lane, known as 'Goggs,' was great for sledding although some children ended up in the stream."

Initial administration seemed to be a highly complex affair, with committees for general management, ladies, finance, entertainment and sports. To fund general maintenance, the chief tenants and landowners in the district were asked to make a donation.

A varied programme of entertainment soon developed, which included a regular cinema show, a welcome supper for soldiers

> "In the past when roads were safer, Church Hill was also a magnet for the children. Sliding on the ice in winter and soapbox go-karts in summer. Great prestige was given to the child with six wheels on his soapbox."

> "Subsidised visits to local swimming pools have allowed practically every child in the latter half of the century to be taught to swim. Cycling proficiency lessons are also provided and in the 1980s the Parish Council incorporated a bicycle circuit into the new playing field at Plott Lane."

returning from the war and a Young Men's Club. The Women's Institute met for regular meetings, the Sunday School took place every Sunday and the Reverend Collier ran a Boy's Club for two nights per week. Whist drives, bazaars, concerts, fancy dress parties and dances all became regular features. The original Whit-Monday Fete became an annual event.

In 1921 a new Management Committee was formed; so enthusiastic were villagers to support their hall that nearly 40 members were elected. While an executive committee of fourteen dealt with general administration, all members were called for special business. One such meeting held on May 7 1926 was obliged to make an emergency decision to postpone the fete because of the General Strike.

Throughout the 1920s, many improvements were made to the building. A kitchen and annex were added and stoves, fire buckets and lamps installed. The annex roof was originally thatched but later tiled to meet fire regulations.

The outbreak of the Second World War in 1939 brought a flurry of wedding receptions and the start of air raid protection and Red Cross meetings. The hall later became a refuge for a number of families made homeless by the bombing of Coventry (see Chapter 10).

By the 1950s the building was also in regular use as a school dining hall and in 1951 Dr McElwain applied for surgery facilities in the annex. Clinics continued to be held into the 1970s.

In more recent times, the hall has been in great demand for an even wider variety of activities, from karate classes to youth clubs, from play groups to plays. The original committee work is now undertaken by the current trustees. The hall is maintained by income from rent and the annual fete, with additional grants from the Parish Council and Borough Council.

In 1999, beneath the facade of cladding, modern emulsion paint and double glazed windows, the original army hut converted in the 1920's still remains. Its preservation is a fitting tribute both to those who died in the First World War and to the hard work of the original Trustees and villagers.

THE FOSSE PLAYING FIELD

Built on approximately five acres of land originally forming part of Yew Tree Farm, the field was purchased by Mr Robert Campion and presented to the village in 1935 in memory of his wife, Alice Houghton Campion. The playing field was officially opened on May 12 1935 by the donor and a stone, fetched from a quarry at Nuneaton, was erected to commemorate the event. In later years, Mr Jack Kennedy, as chairman of the Parish Council, was responsible for equipping the playing area.

The official opening of the Playing Fields, Fosse Way, in May 1937.
The land was donated by Mr R Campion in memory of his wife.

133

THE PLOTT LANE PLAYING FIELD

With the aid of funds drawn from the celebration of the Queen's Silver Jubilee in 1977, a piece of land was purchased by the Parish Council in Plott Lane for a new playing field. This has provided an additional recreational area away from the busy Fosse Way.

PERFORMING ARTS
Choirs

Song and dance have always played a part in village life and the church choir was a strong element of this. Although we have no records for earlier centuries, we do know that only men and boys sang in the parish church choir at the end of the 19th and beginning of the 20th century. A young man of the time remembers that "without a doubt, Stretton boasted the best male choir you could have, filling six or eight pews."

In 1917 the choir consisted of about ten men and twelve boys. By this time social activities stretched beyond the church and the Shoulder of Mutton: a choir outing is recorded in 1914 to the town, with "a visit to a picture show and a good tea."

The two world wars brought a shortage of male voices and a considerable reduction in the size of the choir, which now consisted mainly of ladies, for whom Mr Low Smith of Church Hill purchased a full set of robes. The Reverend Squires conducted the new voices with much enthusiasm and was replaced the 1970s by Reverend Brough, who also had a strong interest in music. A new choir emerged which was eventually mixed. This was in a very relaxed, village style: one member recalls an apprentice organist in the late 1970s who "was only able to play with one hand at choir practice but was wonderful on the trumpet !"

> *"We were paid 2s 6d a year for singing in the choir plus a shilling for weddings and funerals. Our annual outing to Leamington or Rugby was always a big occasion but we would have to walk to Brandon or Marton station first then the whole way back. Sometimes the big boys would let you ride on their shoulders."*

The ladies of the choir in 1948.

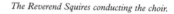

The Reverend Squires conducting the choir.

In 1988, after a successful concert which combined singers from a wide area, it was suggested that All Saints Church should again have a formal choir. A local musician and lecturer, Rosemary Mailey, agreed to be director and twelve singers rehearsed and supported church services twice a month. Their talents were soon taken beyond the services and their first concert took place in the summer of that year, followed by many more. There are now 30 voices in what has become the Stretton Chamber Choir. Their tenth year was marked with a performance of Brahm's Requiem with an orchestra of 13 players and the choir has been invited to sing at many venues, including Bosworth Battlefield, Birmingham NEC, Coventry and Barnstaple. In the summer of 1998 the choir travelled to Italy as guests at a week-long festival to celebrate the battle of Tassera and in 1999 sang in Montbéliard as part of the 10th anniversary celebrations of the French town's association with the village.

Stretton Chamber Choir singing in Como Cathedral on their visit to Italy in August 1998.

"In the early 20th century, Mr Gilbert ran a brass band in which each child played an instrument. The band played at various events and occasions."

"At Christmas time around 1920, one old character would put a gramophone and records into an old pram and go round the village carol singing - Stretton's one-man band."

"We put on sketches and plays and enjoyed it as much as the audience. 'Old George' got very annoyed with us if we didn't do just as he wanted and didn't take things seriously.

He would say, 'Come Emily, shut the piano,' and they would march out. They would always be back the next night and all would be forgiven."

"Mr Austin, the schoolmaster, would sing lovely old ballads at the Old Scholars Association concerts."

Drama

In a county renowned for drama both religious and secular, Stretton has no doubt produced many 'players' throughout the centuries. Our records start in the 1920s and 30s with the Old Scholars' concert parties featuring George Hallett and his wife as conductor and pianist. Talented local artists included Bill and Min Hayden, Roy and Arthur Lewin, Alice Paget, Wal and Pip Richardson and many more.

By now the Village Hall had acquired a full set of staging and concerts of all kinds were also a regular occurrence after the war. Music hall evenings were often held and even the Women's Institute was persuaded to organise plays and sketches.

Stretton on Stage

In 1985, a successful village concert, involving representatives of many village organisations, encouraged a small group of people to form an amateur dramatics group. The organisation was christened Stretton on Stage and is now in its 15th successful year. Its principal aims are to provide entertainment, promote drama and the arts and develop the skills of people of all ages, both on stage and behind the scenes. It currently has approximately

Stretton on Stage's 10th Anniversary Pantomime of Cinderella in 1995.

90 members aged 8 to 70 who have produced a wide range of productions, including around 12 pantomimes or musical shows and 15 plays. With a policy of developing all of its members, it has become a rich source of talent in the area and many have gained sufficient confidence to progress to further opportunities and training in drama, music or technical skills. Presenting an average of three productions a year, the group has raised well over £10,000 for a variety of charitable causes.

SPORT

While sport has become an important part of the leisure industry in the later part of this century, Stretton has recorded a variety of sporting activities for many years.

The Cricket Club

As a true English community, Stretton has seen numerous games of cricket played within its boundaries, although few formal records have survived and clubs have risen and fallen for social and economic reasons.

Perhaps its earliest mark was made by a Stretton cricketer of national fame. William Molyneux Rose a famous bowler in the late 19th century, playing for England with W.G.Grace and renowned as the best lob bowler in the country. He died in Stretton in 1917 and is buried in the churchyard.

> *"During the first world war, there was a sawmill in Frankton Lane. Harry Paget would make you a cricket bat there if you asked him."*

> *"In 1954 George Paget bemoaned the demise of the cricket club because of no pitch. 'Real good team too. I played last year at Ryton and got second highest score.' He was 78."*

Village cricket clubs have played at various locations, notably in a field at the rear of cottages at the top of the lane to Wolston, at The Old Turf (a field at the top of School Lane), a field in Rugby Lane, a paddock at the top of Finacre Lane and, more recently, the Fosse Way playing fields. Members of earlier cricket clubs this century have happy memories of successful matches.

The present Cricket Club has set its sights firmly on the future by establishing a permanent site for their matches. In the winter of 1990, a meeting was called in a move to re-form a club in the village after a long gap. Despite a limited response, it was decided to arrange a match on the school playing fields.

The result was a story worth relating: It was decided with much excitement that the playing strip, previously used for football, should be properly prepared. A tractor was duly borrowed with a heavy agricultural roller about 10 feet (3 metres) wide. After a long struggle bringing the roller from Frankton Lane to the school without demolishing kerbs, walls and gardens, the weight of the roller was found to weigh the tractor down so

The Cricket Team in the late 1940s.

much that extremely deep depressions would be left on the field; the rolling project was abandoned. The strip was ultimately cut with great effort and a 12-inch mower. Whether or not this and the freezing weather affected their performance, Stretton were eventually bowled out for just eleven runs.

Regardless of their early problems, however, a team was entered in the evening 20-Over League for the Rugby area and also arranged fixtures for Sundays. Its home matches were initially played at Princethorpe college but, as interest was now sufficiently great to form a second

Stretton Cricket Team of 1995.

team, agreement was eventually made with the Parish Council to rent the Plott Lane playing field as a permanent ground. Grants were sought to develop facilities, an all-weather strip was laid and a temporary pavilion erected.

Success followed and promotion in the leagues continued, culminating in the team being cup finalists in 1996. The club now has six teams (two junior, two league senior and two senior friendly fixtures teams) and is awaiting planning permission for a permanent pavilion and facilities which, needless to say, include their own mower. With a strong and active social aspect to the club, new members, especially younger ones, are particularly welcome.

Football

Stretton has produced numerous, excellent football teams and has been home to several professional players, including Jesse Quinney and Brian Roberts. The club has operated in various forms throughout the 20th century and, before the opening of the recreation ground and the pavilion on the Fosse Way, used a variety of sites. These included a pitch on the London Road, a further field at the end of Finacre Lane, another on the site of Croft Close and one in Plott Lane. Earlier in the century, club meetings were held at the club

Stretton on Dunsmore football team, winners of runners up medals, 1923-24 season.

Stretton on Dunsmore football team, in the early 1960s prior to the building of the new pavilion in 1963.

house at the Shoulder of Mutton and the two pubs in the centre of the village. So many players and supporters have been involved that it would be impossible to accurately list them all. A selection of photographs collected by Ron Healey, a major contributor to the success of the club from 1948 to 1976, both as player and Club Secretary, will give some idea of the importance of the sport in the village.

In 1996 Stretton Athletic A.F.C. set up a junior section to provide organised football and coaching to children from the village and the surrounding area. More than 25 children immediately registered for training sessions and the club was able to set up teams for under 11s and under 14s. Since that time, its success has grown enormously and in 1999 the club attracted a membership of over 120 children taking part in Saturday morning sessions. There are now five teams competing in local junior leagues.

Stretton Athletic AFC 1996

The junior club is managed by an enthusiastic committee which enjoys considerable support in its fundraising events. As an affiliated member of the Birmingham County Football Association, the club has enlisted the voluntary services of dedicated trainers (currently numbering fourteen), most of whom are qualified as junior team managers and coaches.

In addition to its remarkable rise as one of the best junior clubs in the area, three young players have been invited to attend trials for the Coventry City F.C. Club of Excellence.

A 'veterans' team for the over 35s has also competed with great enthusiasm and no little skill over the past two seasons, in friendly matches and the national Umbro competition, and in keeping with the traditions of previous teams during the last century, the adult team continues to offer excellent hospitality at the Oak and Black Dog.

Tennis

A tennis club successfully operated at Burydyke on the London Road in the 1930s and tennis club dances were frequently held at the Village Hall.

In 1996 an initiative was started to build tennis courts in the village for use by the general public. Suitable land has been located and funds are currently being raised through grants and public donations.

The Ladies Hockey Team

The team was formed in the early 1930's. Girls aged 14-15 upwards were invited to play. The pitch was situated along Plott Lane, on the left and near to the present playing field. They were very successful and played many Coventry teams rarely losing a match.

Other sporting teams and clubs have included tug-of-war, darts, shooting, badminton, dominos and rifle shooting (see Chapter 12).

SOCIAL ORGANISATIONS

Such a busy village has generated innumerable social activities during the last century: sponsored walks, art and craft shows, barn dances, jumble sales, sewing circles and many more. For example, gardening and produce shows were regularly held in the village until the 1970s. In addition to annual and occasional events, the community has also supported a number of important organisations, including a Womens' Guild as early as 1914 and, in 1999 a Cancer Self Help Group.

The Mothers Union

The Mothers Union was formed in 1876 by Mary Sumner and had three objectives: to uphold the sanctity of marriage, to awaken in all mothers the sense of their great responsibility in the training of their children as future parents and to organise in every place a band of mothers who would unite in prayer. It became a world-wide organisation. The Stretton and Princethorpe branch recorded excellent attendance for many years and was normally led by the current vicar's wife.

No church function in the village would have been complete without a contribution from the mothers of the village: the group performed practical functions, such as cleaning and decorating the church for festivals, and took part in social events, both for church fairs and bazaars and in the form of garden parties and outings.

In latter years, however, the change in women's lifestyles and status led to a drop in attendance and it was with great regret that in 1995 closure became inevitable and its last Enrolling Member, Freda Leaver, handed over the Stretton service books to the Mothers Union Office.

The Women's Institute

The 'W.I.' was a national organisation formed to educate women living in rural areas on health and hygiene matters, homemaking and self-improvement.

Stretton W.I. was first established during the 1930s, its first President being Mrs Lister-Kaye. During the second World War, however, it was suspended to allow members to help with the war effort. In 1946 the village branch was re-formed under a new President, Mrs Bass, and supported by some 50 to 60 members. A new spirit of camaraderie and fun became part of the post-war meetings. Although the original programme of activities was similar to today's, members now attend national and local events and listen to a wide range of speakers. Worldwide issues and technology are

Women's Institute outing to Josiah Wedgwood in the early 1960s.

now very much part of the modern organisation, as is demonstrated by its new motto "Today's women working for tomorrow's world."

Stretton Ladies Fellowship

The All Saints Young Wives group was formed in January 1966 with twelve members and developed close links with the Mothers Union. During the first year, with emphasis less on homecrafts than other ladies' organisations, a number of speakers presented topics as varied as The Church of England Children's Society and First Aid in the Home.

Its aim was also to provide community support and after the first AGM members agreed to give help when requested at village functions. The name was later changed to Stretton Wives Fellowship and the decision made to hold meetings in members' homes to encourage the closeness of the group. The first of many Open Meetings (on Guide Dogs for the Blind) was held in June 1969 in the Village Hall, with refreshments costing a hefty 6d.

141

25th Anniversary of the Ladies Fellowship.

In the early years, although there was no age limit, the majority of members had young families and subjects reflected this: in September 1969, Mrs Gardener spoke about The Television Set and Your Family, and a baby-sitting scheme was organised for those who were interested. Such was the focus on young family life that the date of the 1988 A.G.M. was urgently changed because the chairwoman was due to give birth.

By 1971, the programme was more varied, and annual outings were arranged to places such as Draycote Water, Kenilworth Castle and local theatres. In 1973, the Ladies Fellowship decided to become disaffiliated from the Mothers Union but keep its close links with the Church, a link which endures today.

The group continues to play an active part in village life, taking part in the flower rota for the church, the Christian Aid Collection in May, an annual Cake Sale for the Children's Society, refreshments for Church functions and help to those in the village who need support. One particularly important feature in the Ladies Fellowship programme of events is the Annual Harvest Supper, referred to in Chapter 13.

In July 1989, the group name was changed again, to Stretton Ladies Fellowship, to encompass all women. In 1999 there are more than 30 members.

The Over Sixties Club

The Club's first meeting was held in 1964 and attended by 34 members with Mrs B Gullick being the first chairman. By the next year membership had increased to 60 and members were asked to pay a subscription of 4 shillings (20p).

The first fund raising event was a 'sale of work', which graduated to an Autumn Fair in the Village Hall. This was a popular event in the Village Calendar for at least 25 years but in more recent times, the main fund raising event has been a Summer Garden Party.

The format of the meetings has hardly changed over the years: a friendly chat with tea and biscuits with perhaps a game of cards or bingo. A number of interesting outings are arranged throughout the year, including a Christmas Lunch.

The annual membership fee is now £2.50. The Club is affiliated to Age Concern and receives regular updates on help and helplines which are available to senior citizens and their carers.

The Friends of the Pays de Montbéliard

In May 1989 a large group of residents of the village, mainly members of the All Saints Choir at that time, travelled to France to take part in musical events at the Protestant church in the centre of the town of Montbéliard, in Eastern

The Diari Folklore Group on the village green, 12th July 1998.

France. The occasion was to be the start of a highly successful 'twinning' arrangement. In the summer of that year, as a result of contact between Irène Deasley (Peugeot UK) and Pasteur Yves Parrand, two associations were formed to promote friendship between the people of the two communities: 'L'Association des Amis du Mai Anglais' in France and 'The Friends of the Pays de Montbéliard' in Stretton.

Later that year a French delegation was welcomed in the village, staying with local families and enjoying reciprocal hospitality.

The association has encouraged regular exchanges between the two communities, with musical events in both countries, group visits and private visits. No formal membership or language skill is required. Highlights have included visits from France by English classes and a local folk group, the DIARI. The twin associations celebrated their tenth anniversary in 1999 when a delegation of 60 people from Stretton gave a celebratory concert and performed a specially written English pantomime at an anniversary reception in Montbéliard.

The Duck Race

Since the initial idea, conceived by a group of gentlemen in the Oak and Black Dog, of a fundraising event in 1987 to benefit the cancer ward at Walsgrave Hospital and the mammography appeal at St Cross Hospital, the Duck Race has become an annual event. The first race took place November 1988 with an armada of sponsored plastic ducks dramatically released along the brook in the centre of the village, Ten years later a total of £29,170 had been raised for a wide variety of local charities, large and small.

The annual 'Duck Race.'

Scouting

The Scout Movement was started at the beginning of the 1900s by Robert Baden Powell, whose father was the first cousin of the Reverend Harry Townsend Powell, vicar at Stretton from 1830-1855. Perhaps influenced by this link, scouting was established early in the village. The first scoutmaster, H. Chater, and his assistant, T. Finch were not issued with warrants until 1914 but the register is marked 'old warrant of March 1910, new warrant issued March 1914.' By 1916 there were 23 scouts but the troop was suspended because of the 1st World War.

> *"We are pleased to learn that both our Assistant Scoutmasters (now serving in the Army) have gained promotion."*
>
> *"The Scout Troup continues its winter work for badges, including carpentry, bee-keeping and horsemanship. Troup inspection October 6th. Full dress."*
>
> From the Parish Magazine 1914

No further mention is made of the Stretton Troop in early records at Baden Powell House but they continued to be active throughout the 2nd World War. One of the leaders, Mr Richardson, was grandfather of one of the present leaders, Ian Coleman,.

In the early 1950s, the group disbanded but in 1968 the arrival of a trained cub leader, Kay Craddock, led to the formation of a Cub Pack for boys aged 8 to 10. Shortly afterwards natural progression led to the formation of a new Scout troop.

The Brownies in the late 1980s.

The new group has continued to run successfully under a series of leaders and committees, instigating not only traditional camping and hiking events but barn dances and 'sportaculars' for fundraising. 1986 saw the arrival of the Beavers, a new branch for 5-8 year olds. In 1995 the Venture Scout unit for young people of both sexes aged 15 to 21 added a new dimension.

Stretton Girl Guides in the 1930s.

144

Girl Guides

In parallel to the Boy Scout groups, there have been a succession of Girl Guide and Ranger companies in Stretton, Princethorpe and Ryton from as early as the 1930s. The units were in operation until the 1980s.

While there are currently no guides in the village, Brownie and Rainbow packs, which were added for younger girls, continue to this day.

Youth Groups

From the very earliest days of the Village Hall, clubs and groups for the young people in the community have been so numerous that it would be impossible to mention them all. Memories of the 1930s include a young men's club which was held at the Vicarage by the Reverend Collier, when "Troublesome lads were encouraged to play billiards to stop them being a nuisance in the village". The current youth group was established in 1996 and offers a range of activities including outings, music, a pool table, darts and soft ball. With the aid of a grant in 1997 the group applied their artistic skills to decorating the bus shelter with a mural depicting local landmarks.

With the church as a focal point of a rural community, Sunday school classes, under a variety of titles, have no doubt been held in the village for centuries. The introduction of a more relaxed form of church 'club', such as Children's Church and Assets in the 1980s and 1990s, provided a less formal atmosphere for young people of different ages. A Sunday Club currently operates at the church twice a month for children of various age groups.

Parent & Toddler and Play Groups have also been held at the Village Hall for many years.

PENDULUM

Perhaps the main link between leisure activities in many English villages is the parish magazine. At the beginning of the 20th century, a diocesan publication was distributed in Stretton containing general religious stories and comments to which local news had been added. Advertisements were also a regular feature. This was later replaced by a parochial newsletter for All Saints Church. The first edition of a magazine specifically for Stretton and Princethorpe, and bearing the name 'Pendulum', was published in September 1965 at a cost of 2s 6d per year. The design of the original front by John Williams, a resident of the village, was intended to suggest "varying shades of opinion in the parish, with the church at the centre of all on a white ground (the biblical colour for victory)." The cover is now produced in a variety of colours but retains the central image of the church.

All Saints Church, Stretton-on-Dunsmore with St. Cuthbert's, Princethorpe

Pendulum

Number 394

October 1999

The modern magazine, essential in such a busy community, continues to provide extensive information for the two villages and is distributed every month.

15

INTO THE MILLENNIUM
VIEWS OF THE VILLAGE

The past fifty years have seen many changes in Stretton on Dunsmore. Modern mechanised farming significantly reduced the number of people engaged in agricultural work whilst the development of engineering industries in nearby towns created alternative employment. These changes initially caused some people to leave the village but development of housing and improvements in transport soon reversed the trend and encouraged both newcomers and existing residents to commute to work in nearby towns.

Housing in Stretton grew to meet the needs and demands of modern post-war Britain. Many older buildings have remained, intact and improved, but poor sanitation and conditions led to a large number of cottages being demolished. These were replaced by new houses along the Fosse, in Croft Close, Hill Crescent and in Plott Lane. Modern homes and bungalows now stand on the site of the Well Head cottages and Parrott's House. Traces of the old Manor House have disappeared under Manor Drive and new developments have become well established on old quarry sites at Knob Hill, Bartletts Hill and School Lane. In latter years small estates were also built on 'green' sites at Meadow Close, Orchard Way and Squires Road.

The combination of old with new has created much demand for housing within the parish. In addition to housing needs, rural traditions have been fostered and retained by older residents while newcomers have brought young families to inject new vigour into a friendly and active community.

Wherever the place of work, the village still provides a peaceful homecoming after a hard day and the green, the church, the pubs and the old cottages still create a pleasant picture for both the resident and the visitor. Stretton on Dunsmore faces the new Millennium with the knowledge that, with careful control of bricks, mortar and countryside, it will not only survive but continue to thrive as it has for more than a thousand years.

"We fell in love with Stretton on a grey November day because of the green and the bridge over the stream. We were looking for a community, with a school, a shop and a pub (a post office and second pub were a bonus). Everyone told us what a nice place it was to live in, with plenty of activities going on and friendly people. So we bought a house on a modern estate, looking out onto a green, well away from the main roads. That was 1990 and I still feel privileged as I sit in my study, with a view of the trees and the church, listening to the lambs, a cuckoo and skylarks in summer. People ask us whether we'll move when we retire but we are perfectly happy here."
Anne Langley, a new resident

"Little did I think, when I came, as a newcomer, for a quiet drink on the village green, that I would still be here 50 years later! It's home - we would never leave."
Steve Smith, long-term resident

"There have been many changes over the years and village people do not always like change forced upon them. I remember, as a very young girl, standing with my brother watching a bulldozer destroying our den and pond on the site of the new Manor Drive.
I cried buckets - but several years later my brother's future wife moved in.
As children, my younger sister, Gillian, and I picked blackberries and buttercups in fields alongside Plott Lane. Then along came the bulldozer and Orchard Way was built. I was very upset about this. But some of my dearest friends live there now.
We played on the site of the old camp in School Lane, climbing banks strewn with dog roses and playing hide-and-seek in brambles and long grass. Then along came that old bulldozer and a new school was built. My children went there and I have worked there for several years.
We had pony rides in the fields in Church Hill but bulldozing was spreading like wildfire and soon two bungalows appeared.
My parents retired to one of them a few years ago.
Another little girl plays in our old summer-house and my parents' butcher's shop is now someone's sitting room. My own children have grown and still come home to check that their secret dens in the Meadows have not been destroyed. I know just how they feel - but maybe some changes are not that bad after all!"
Mary Pinchen,
daughter of John Anderton, last butcher in the village

"We really enjoy living in Stretton with its easy access to a number of towns and many picturesque places to visit. We also enjoy living on the Fosse. We have a lifetime of happy memories of our children growing up here. Now they bring our grandchildren to visit. We have had good times in Stretton on Dunsmore."
Freda & Eddy Leaver, long-term residents

"There are many reasons why I like living in Stretton on Dunsmore but the main one is the friendship that is here between everyone. There are many organisations that involve many people from the village; these organisations join up the community of Stretton to make the village what it is. There are also a fair few people of the teen age to be friends with and many activities for us.
It is a great place to be and there is always something to do."
Emma Hinton,
a teenager brought up in the village

Although I was not born in Stretton, I have spent most of my 95 years in and around the village and have many happy memories. I have seen many changes and take pleasure in the fact that it is still a thriving community. I am delighted that this record has now been compiled."
Harold Campion, one of the oldest residents

149

THE PAROCHIAL CHURCH COUNCIL

Vicar	Rev. Christine Pollard
Church Wardens	Thelma Cain, Brian Clay
Secretary	Vicky Lundberg
Treasurer	Alan Parsons
Deanery Synod	Paulin Clay, Sheelagh March
Members	Andrew Freeman, Michelle Hall, Peter Lewis, John Simmonds, Janet Simmonds, Louise Simmonds, Paul Simmons

THE PARISH COUNCIL

Chairman	Ian Smith
Vice Chairman	John Simmonds
Clerk:	Sarah Miles
Councillors	Rodney Boneham, Barry McKenna, Jesse Quinney, Bryan Sapwell, Frances Ravenhall, Neil Thompson
Borough Councillors	
Knightlow Ward	Bill Shields, Ron Ravenhall

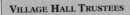

SCENES FROM THE END OF THE MILLENNIUM

153

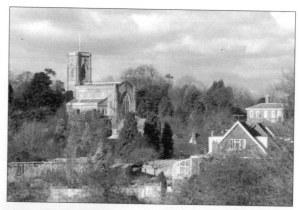

AN HISTORIC WALK AROUND
STRETTON ON DUNSMORE

We hope that the book will inspire you to take a closer look at the way the village has developed over the last one thousand years. A walk map has been designed to include the main points of interest, starting at Well Head. The route is two and a half miles in length, using roads and public footpaths. It returns to the same spot and can be shortened by leaving at Point 17. Look for the sites listed below and use the index at the back of the book to find further information on their history.

1. Well Head - possible site of original settlement
2. The Surgery
3. The original school building, now 64 & 66 Brookside
4. The Oak & Black Dog
5. Yew Tree Hall
6. The old bakehouse
7. Brookside Stores & Post Office
8. The site of the first Methodist Chapel
9. Site of the old Manor House
10. The Shoulder of Mutton
11. Site of the Pool Yard (moat & orchard). Now private land.
12. Church Farm
13. The Manor House
14. All Saints Church & site of old church
15. The old vicarage, now Stretton House
16. The Village Hall
17. Moor Farm
18. Dunsmore House, 17th century cottage
19. Manor Farm
20. Old gypsum workings, below modern housing
21. Site of Victorian school
22. Methodist Chapel - now disused
23. Site of the Plott, water pump & allotments
24. The new school

The Walk

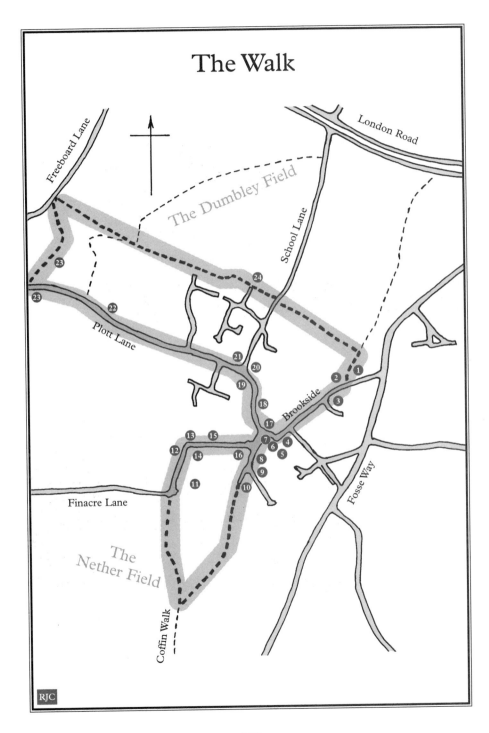

INDEX